Century 21®
Computer Applications and Keyboarding
NINTH EDITION

Australia · Brazil · Japan · Korea · Mexico · Singapore · Spain · United Kingdom · United States

Style Manual: Century 21® Computer Applications and Keyboarding, Ninth Edition

Vice President of Editorial, Business: Jack W. Calhoun

Vice President/Editor-in-Chief: Karen Schmohe

Acquisitions Editor: Jane Congdon

Sr. Developmental Editor: Dave Lafferty

Consulting Editor: Jean Findley, Custom Editorial Productions, Inc.

Marketing Manager: Valerie Lauer

Sr. Content Project Manager: Martha Conway

Sr. Manufacturing Buyer: Charlene Taylor

Production Service: GGS Book Services.

Sr. Art Director: Tippy McIntosh

Cover Designer: Grannan Graphic Design Ltd.

Cover Image: Grannan Graphic Design Ltd.

For product information and technology assistance, contact us at
Cengage Learning Customer & Sales Support, 1-800-354-9706

For permission to use material from this text or product,
submit all requests online at **www.cengage.com/permissions**
Further permissions questions can be emailed to
permissionrequest@cengage.com

Microsoft and Windows are registered trademarks of Microsoft Corporation in the U.S. and/or other countries.

The names of all products mentioned herein are used for identification purposes only and may be trademarks or registered trademarks of their respective owners. South-Western disclaims any affiliation, association, connection with, sponsorship, or endorsement by such owners.

ISBN-13: 978-0-538-44916-8

ISBN-10: 0-538-44916-0

South-Western Cengage Learning
5191 Natorp Boulevard
Mason, OH 45040
USA

Cengage Learning products are represented in Canada by Nelson Education, Ltd.

For your course and learning solutions, visit **school.cengage.com**
Visit our company website at **www.cengage.com**

Printed in the United States of America
1 2 3 4 5 6 7 13 12 11 10 09

Preface

The *Century 21 Style Manual* supplements *Century 21 Computer Applications and Keyboarding, Ninth Edition*, and *Century 21 Computer Keyboarding, Ninth Edition*. It contains selected information from the textbook. Thus, the *Style Manual* is convenient to use alongside the textbook or by itself, long after completing the keyboarding/computer applications course.

Students will find this manual useful in preparing business documents and reports for school, personal, and office purposes. Included in the manual are basic word processing features and formatting styles for business letters, memos, e-mail, reports, tables, and other documents. Also included is a section on employment documents. Style guides for capitalization, number expression, punctuation, basic grammar, confusing words, and proofreaders' marks are included to aid students in preparing all types of documents.

The *Century 21 Style Manual* retains its value long after the school years by continuing to serve as a personal reference and on-the-job guide to quality document processing. The manual is available in printed form and on the Web at www.cengage.com/school/keyboarding/C21.

Table of Contents

Word Processing Features

Word processing software offers a variety of features and commands that enable users to create attractive business documents easily and efficiently. This section provides a brief description of many basic features that can be found in most word processing software programs.

BASIC COMMANDS

Basic commands include the operations necessary to view, save, print, and close a document.

- **Open.** Displays lists of folders and files (documents). Use this command to locate a desired document and open (display) it on the screen.
- **Save/Save As.** Saves a document on a disk while leaving a copy of it on the screen. Use *Save As* the first time a document is saved (give it a filename) and to rename a document. Use *Save* to save a revised document without renaming it.
- **Print Preview.** Shows a document as it will look when printed, including multiple pages in one view.
- **Print.** Prints documents. Select print options and settings (Print dialog box) before printing.
- **Close.** Removes a document from the display screen. If the document has not been saved, you will be prompted to save it before closing.

EDITING FEATURES

Editing features allow the user to locate, revise, correct, and rearrange text in a document.

- **Copy.** Copies selected text so it can be placed in another location, leaving the original text unchanged.
- **Cut.** Removes selected text from the current location.
- **Paste.** Places selected text that has been copied or cut at another location.
- **Find.** Locates a specified keystroke, word, or phrase in a document. Available Find options include:
  - Find only occurrences that match the specified case.
  - Find only whole words containing the specified text.
  - Find all forms of a specified word.
  - Find specified text using the asterisk (*) and question mark (?) as wildcard (unspecified) characters.

- **Replace.** Finds a specified keystroke, word, or phrase, and then replaces it with another keystroke, word, or phrase. All occurrences of the specified text can be replaced at one time, or replacements can be made individually (selectively).

- **Select.** Highlights text on which various operations may be performed. Use the mouse and/or key combinations to select text. Once selected, the text can be bolded, underlined, italicized, deleted, copied, moved, printed, saved, etc.

- **Spell-Check.** Checks words, documents, or parts of documents for misspellings.

- **Undo.** Reverses the last change made in the text. This feature restores moved text to its original location.

- **Redo.** Reverses the last Undo action.

- **Typeover.** Replaces existing text with newly keyed text (also called *Overstrike* or *Overtype*).

ENHANCEMENT FEATURES

Enhancement features improve the appearance of a document and/or emphasize important words, phrases, or sentences.

- **Bold.** Prints text darker than other copy as it is keyed. Bold may be added after text has been keyed by first selecting the text.

- **Borders.** Adds a border to any or all sides of a page, paragraph, or column, as well as to a table or a cell within a table. Page border options may include small pictures. Borders not only enhance appearance, but also make text easier to read by emphasizing certain passages. Borders are most effective when used sparingly.

- **Bullets.** Highlights each item in a list with a heavy dot or other character, as demonstrated in this list of features. Bullets add visual interest and emphasis.

- **Change Case.** Changes capitalization. The lowercase option changes all selected text to lowercase; the UPPERCASE option changes selected text to all capitals. The Sentence case option capitalizes the first letter of the first word, and the Title Case option capitalizes the first letter of each selected word.

- **Drop Cap.** Formats paragraphs to begin with a large dropped capital letter. Drop caps are objects (pictures) that can be formatted and sized.

- **Font.** Consists of the *typeface, style, size,* and any *effects* used. Font features may be changed before or after text is keyed. The number and size of fonts available depends on the software and printer used.

  - **Typeface.** Refers to the design of the characters. Examples include Times New Roman, `Courier New`, and **Arial**.

- **Styles.** Include bold and italic.
- **Size.** Measured in *points* such as 10 point or 12 point. One point is about $\frac{1}{72}$ of an inch.
- **Effect.** Added to give text a special look. Examples of effects are shadow, emboss, and small caps. Effects should be used infrequently.

■ **Italic.** Prints letters that slope up toward the right. Italic may be added after text has been keyed by first selecting the text.

■ **Numbering.** Shows the proper order of a series of steps or items. Use numbers instead of bullets whenever the order of items is important.

■ **Shading.** Adds color or patterns to paragraphs or table cells to emphasize them and focus the reader's attention on the contents.

■ **Superscript.** Places text slightly higher than other text on a line. Superscript is commonly used for footnotes and endnotes, and for mathematical formulas and equations.

■ **Underline.** Underlines text as it is keyed. An underline may be added after text has been keyed by first selecting the text.

■ **Watermark.** Prints any desired text or graphics behind the main text on document pages.

FORMATTING FEATURES

Formatting features change the arrangement, or layout, of pages. These features include aligning text vertically and horizontally, indenting and hyphenating text, and changing margins and line spacing.

■ **Alignment.** Refers to the horizontal position of a line of text (also called *justification*).
- Use **left** alignment to start text at the left margin (even left margin).
- Use **right** alignment to align text at the right margin (even right margin).
- Use **center** alignment to center text between the left and right margins.
- Use **justify** alignment for even left and right margins.

■ **Center Page.** Centers text between top and bottom margins of a page. This feature leaves an equal (or nearly equal) amount of white space above and below text. Inserting two hard returns below the last keyed line gives centered documents a better appearance.

■ **Hyphenation.** Automatically divides (hyphenates) words that would normally wrap to the next line. When used with left-aligned text, hyphenation makes the right margin less ragged, making text more attractive.

- **Indent.** Moves text away from the left or right margin.
  - **Left indent (paragraph indent)** moves the text one tab stop to the right (usually 0.5"), away from the left margin.
  - **Hanging indent** moves all but the first line of a paragraph 0.5" (one tab stop) to the right. Hanging indent is commonly used on bibliographies and reference pages.
- **Line Spacing.** Changes the amount of blank space between lines of text.
- **Margins.** Changes the amount of blank space at the top, bottom, right, and/or left edges of a page. Default margin settings are not the same for all software.
- **Page Break.** Inserts a *soft page break* automatically when the current page is full. A *hard page break* can be inserted manually to start a new page before the current page is full.
- **Tab.** Aligns text according to the type of tab set. By default, most word processing software programs have left tabs already set at half-inch (0.5") intervals from the left margin. These preset tabs can be cleared and reset.
  - **Left** tabs, commonly used to align words, align text evenly at the left by placing the keyed text to the right of the tab setting.
  - **Right** tabs, commonly used to align whole numbers, align text evenly at the right by placing the keyed text to the left of the tab setting.
  - **Decimal** tabs align numbers at the decimal point, regardless of the number of places before or after the decimal point.
  - **Dot Leader** tabs automatically place dot leaders (. . . .) between columns of designated text. The leaders lead the reader's eyes from text in the left column to text in the right column.
- **Text Wrapping.** Positions text in relation to an inserted object (graphic). Text may appear above and below, around, behind, or in front of an object.
- **Widow/Orphan.** Ensures that the first line of a paragraph does not appear by itself at the bottom of a page (orphan line) or that the last line of a paragraph does not appear by itself at the top of a page (widow line).

INSERT FEATURES

Various commands on the Insert menu are used to add page numbers, dates, headers, footers, and footnotes and to insert symbols, clip art, files, pictures, shapes, text boxes, and word art.

- **Shapes.** Adds a variety of shapes (rectangles, stars, banners, arrows, flow chart symbols, etc.) to a document.
- **Clip Art.** Drawings, pictures, sounds, and video clips can be inserted into documents. A collection of clip art files is provided with word processing software; additional clip art can be purchased or downloaded from the Internet.

- **Date.** Automatically inserts the date into a document. Some software contains an Update option that automatically replaces the previous date with the current date each time the document is opened or printed.

- **Footnote and Endnote.** Identifies sources quoted or paraphrased in the text or gives extra information about the main text. Word processing software automatically positions and prints each footnote at the bottom of the same page as the reference to it. It prints endnotes on a separate page at the end of a report. When footnotes or endnotes are edited, added, or deleted, the software feature automatically makes the necessary changes in numbering, formatting, and page breaks.

- **Header and Footer.** Adds text (such as a chapter title, date, filename, or name of a person or company) or graphic (a company logo, for example) in the top margin (header) or bottom margin (footer) of a page. Headers or footers often include page numbers.

- **Page Numbers.** Places page numbers in a specified location on printed pages.
  - Most software contains a variety of numbering styles from which to choose: Arabic numerals (1, 2, 3), lowercase Roman numerals (i, ii, iii), uppercase Roman numerals (I, II, III), uppercase letters (A, B, C), and lowercase letters (a, b, c).
  - Numbers can be placed at the top or bottom of the page, and aligned at the left margin, center, or right margin.
  - The **Hide** or **Suppress** option keeps the page number from appearing on a specified page.

- **Text Boxes.** Frequently used for labels or callouts in a document. Once a text box is inserted in a document, it can be formatted, resized, and moved.

- **Word Art.** Changes text into a graphic object. Most word processing software programs have a word art gallery that contains predefined styles such as curved or stretched text.

MISCELLANEOUS FEATURES

This group contains features included in most word processing software that make the keying task easier and more efficient.

- **AutoFormat.** Automatically formats headings, bulleted and numbered lists, borders, numbers, symbols, and so on as a document is keyed. **Table AutoFormat** applies borders, shading, font effects, etc., to tables.

- **AutoCorrect.** Automatically corrects many common keying, spelling, and grammatical errors. It can also insert certain text, graphics, and symbols automatically.

- **AutoComplete.** Inserts entire items such as dates and **AutoText** (stored phrases) when a few identifying characters are keyed.

- **Macro.** Allows the user to save (record) keystrokes and/or commands for retrieval (playback) later. Macros save time by eliminating repetitive keying and formatting.

- **Show.** Displays marks in text showing where tabs, spaces, and hard returns are inserted. Being able to see these marks helps when editing a document or solving formatting problems. The marks do not print.

- **Split Window.** Displays a document in two panes, each with its own scroll bars. This feature can be useful when copying text between parts of a long document, or when it is necessary to see text not visible in the window where you are keying.

- **Zoom.** Increases or decreases the size of text and amount of a page appearing on the screen. Zoom out (a rate below 100%) to see more of a page and smaller text; zoom in (a rate above 100%) to see less page area and larger text.

SPECIAL FEATURES

The word processing features listed below are used to create specific kinds of documents.

- **Merge.** Combines information from two files into one merged file. The feature is often used to merge a form letter (main document) with a name and address file (data source) to create a personalized letter (merged file) to each recipient in the data source file.

- **Newspaper-Style Columns.** Divides a page into two or more side-by-side columns to create pamphlets, leaflets, brochures, and newsletters. The columns may be equal or unequal width. As the document is keyed, text fills a column before moving to the next column. Often, newspaper-style columns need to be *balanced* (equal or nearly equal in length). The desired balance can be achieved by inserting *column breaks* as needed.

- **Outline.** Automatically labels each topic (paragraph) with a number or letter. The alphanumeric outlining system uses Roman and Arabic numbers and capital and lowercase letters. For example, Level 1 items might be labeled *I, II, III,* etc. Level 2 would be *A, B, C,* etc., and Level 3 would be labeled *1, 2, 3,* etc.

- **Styles.** Applies a predefined set of formatting options to text to add consistency to a document.

- **Table.** Creates a grid for arranging information in rows and columns. A table can be used to summarize information and to arrange it into easily identifiable categories. *Note:* Table features are discussed in the Tables section of this manual.

- **Web Page.** Creates a new blank Web page in the document window. The file is saved in HTML format so it can be viewed in a Web browser.

- **E-Mail.** Creates a new e-mail message in the document window and sends the document as the body of the e-mail.

INPUT TECHNOLOGIES

- **Speech Recognition.** Speech recognition software enables computers to understand spoken words. The user speaks words and commands into a microphone attached to the computer, and the software converts them into word processing documents.

- **Tablet PC.** A type of notebook computer that provides a writing tablet rather than a keyboard where the user can input handwritten notes into the word processing program.

- **Digital Imaging.** A number of different devices provide ways to input documents or photos for use in word processing programs. *Scanners* convert paper documents into digital images, and *digital cameras* create photos as digital images rather than images on film.

- **Personal Digital Assistant (PDA).** A small hand-held computer-like device designed to store information such as a calendar and an address book. Many PDAs offer Internet and e-mail access as well as other enhancements. Information such as addresses, notes, and documents can be exchanged between a PDA and personal computer.

- **Smart Phone.** In addition to its cell phone capabilities, a smart phone allows the user to store an address book and calendar, send and receive e-mail, and synchronize information such as contacts, e-mail, and appointments with a personal computer.

Business Documents

This section covers the formatting of a variety of business documents including business and personal-business letters, envelopes, interoffice memorandums, e-mail messages, reports, and tables. Information includes the formatting and features of the documents as well as illustrations and models.

BUSINESS LETTERS

The basic parts and standard formatting of business letters and envelopes are presented with accompanying illustrations.

BASIC LETTER PARTS

Letterhead. A letterhead contains the name and address of an organization or person. A variety of additional information can be included, such as the telephone number, fax number, e-mail address, list of company officers, and a logo. The letterhead, which is designed to stand out from the text of the letter, is usually preprinted and does not need to be keyed.

Date. The only acceptable date style for letters is month/day/year (*November 14, 2009*), with the month spelled out. Most word processing programs enter and update the date automatically if it is inserted using the Date feature. Key the date 2" from the top of the page, or a DS below a letterhead that is more than 2" deep.

Letter address. Key the receiver's name and address SS, with a minimum of three lines and a maximum of six lines. If the default line spacing in your software is 1.15", you must SHIFT + ENTER after each line of the letter address in order to achieve single spacing. For U.S. addresses, the last line must contain only three elements: city (never abbreviated), state (always two-letter USPS abbreviation), and ZIP+4. The letter address should be the same as the delivery address on the envelope. Begin the address a DS below the date. Key a personal title (*Ms., Mr., Mrs.*) or a professional title (*Dr., Senator*) before the receiver's name. Insert one space between the state and the ZIP code.

Salutation. Key the salutation (greeting) one line below the letter address. Only the title and last name appear in the salutation unless the title is not known and the gender of the addressee is difficult to determine— for example, *Leslie Kennedy*. Then the salutation would read *Dear Leslie Kennedy*.

February 25, 20--

↓2

Ms. Marilyn Lombard
2539 W. Fifth Avenue
San Francisco, CA 94101-3399
↓1
Dear Ms. Lombard

Body. Begin the body (message) of the letter one line below the salutation. Single-space each paragraph with a DS between paragraphs.

Complimentary close. Key the complimentary close (farewell) one line below the body of the letter. If two words are used (*Sincerely yours*), capitalize only the first word.

Name of the writer. Key the name of the writer (sender) two lines below the complimentary close. Generally the personal title of the writer is not included; however, a title can precede the name if a female prefers (*Mrs., Miss, Ms.*) or if the gender of the writer is unclear (*Mr. Leslie Kennedy*). A business title or department may be added below the name of the writer.

Reference initials. If someone other than the writer keys the letter, add the keyboard operator's initials in lowercase letters at the left margin two lines below the writer's name, title, or department.

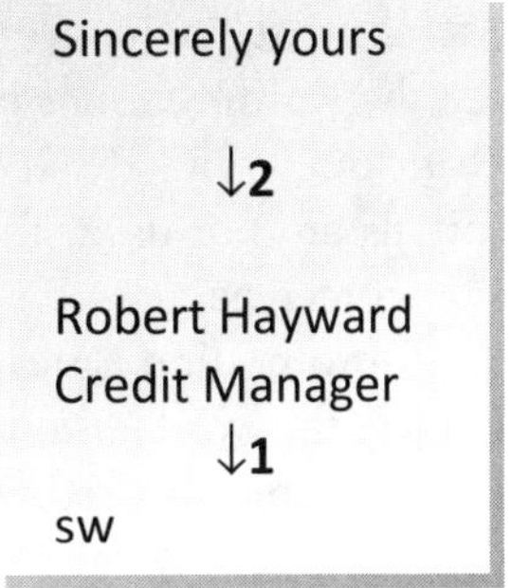

SPECIAL LETTER PARTS

In addition to the basic parts, a business letter may include special letter parts as described below.

Mailing and addressee notations. Mailing notations such as REGISTERED or SPECIAL DELIVERY and addressee notations such as CONFIDENTIAL and PERSONAL may be included in a letter. Key these notations in ALL CAPS one line below the date and one line above the mailing address.

Attention line. If the writer does not know the name of the receiver of the letter or is writing the letter to an organization, an attention line is keyed as the first line of the letter address. For example, *Attention Director of Human Resources* would be keyed on the first line; the company name would be keyed on the second line. When an attention line is used, the salutation should read *Ladies and Gentlemen.*

Subject line. A subject line (optional) is used to identify the main topic discussed in the letter. Key the subject line in ALL CAPS one line below the salutation.

Mr. Robert Anderson
3453 First Street
Cincinnati, OH 45230-9734
↓1
Dear Mr. Anderson
↓1
COMPANY POLICIES
↓1

Attachment/Enclosure notation. If another document is stapled or clipped to a letter, the word *Attachment* is keyed one line below the reference initials. If a document is included with the letter but not attached, the word *Enclosure* is used. If reference initials are not used, the Attachment or Enclosure notation is keyed one line below the writer's name.

If more than one enclosure is included, the word *Enclosures* or *Enclosures #* (see example) is used. Some companies prefer to identify each enclosure so there is no uncertainty over what is included with the letter.

db
↓1
Enclosures 2

Copy notation. A copy notation indicates that a copy of the letter is being sent to someone besides the addressee. Key *c* followed by the name(s) of the person(s) who are to receive a copy. Place the copy notation one line below the enclosure notation, or if no enclosure is included, one line below the reference initials.

Sometimes the writer of the letter wants to send a copy to someone without disclosing this to the addressee of the letter. In this case, key *bc* (blind copy) followed by the name(s). The blind copy notation is keyed on every copy, but not on the original letter.

tp
↓1
Enclosure
↓1
c Mary Albertson

Keyed on original and copy

mp
↓1
bc Michael Blackburn

Keyed on copy only

Postscript. A postscript may be used to emphasize some point discussed in the letter or to add a personal note. This optional part, the last item on the page, is keyed one line below the reference initials or attachment/enclosure or copy notation if these two parts are included. Omit the postscript abbreviation (*P.S.*).

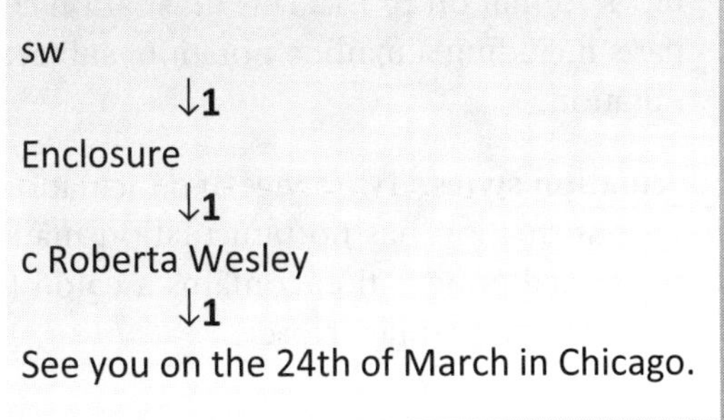

PERSONAL-BUSINESS LETTERS

A letter written by an individual concerning business of a personal nature is called a **personal-business letter**. All the parts of a business letter are included, with one exception: The letterhead is replaced with a return address. A personal-business letter is printed on plain paper with the writer's address keyed 2" from the top of the page at the left margin. The return address consists of one line for the street address and one line for the city, state, and ZIP code. The date is keyed directly below the city, state, and ZIP code.

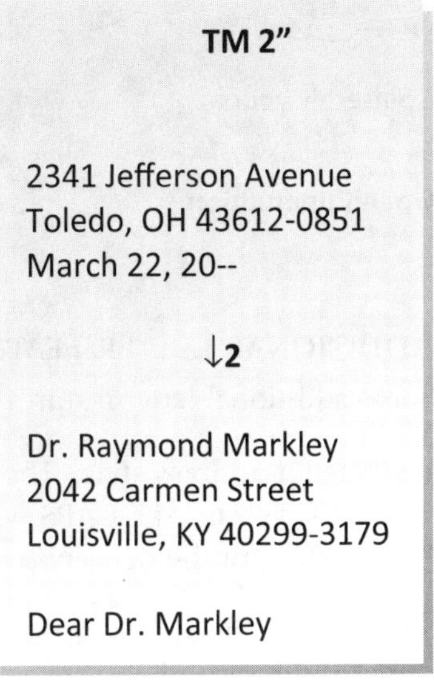

LETTER FORMATS

Business and personal-business letters are arranged in varying formats and styles. These variations are described below.

Margins. Letters are formatted with 1" left and right margins, a 2" top margin, and a 1" bottom margin. Instead of a 2" top margin, letters may be centered vertically using the Center Page feature.

Formats. Business letters are formatted in two basic styles: block and modified block.

- **Block** format arranges all letter parts at the left margin. The paragraphs are not indented. Refer to the illustration of a personal-business letter in block format on p. 14.

- **Modified block** format places the date and the closing lines (complimentary close, writer's name, and title) beginning near the horizontal center of the page instead of at the left margin. The default tab nearest to the center may be used to place the date and closing lines. The first line of each paragraph may be blocked at the left margin or indented 0.5". See the illustration of a letter in modified block format on p. 15. This illustration contains several special business letter parts including a mailing notation, subject line, enclosure notation, and copy notation.

Punctuation styles. Two styles of punctuation are commonly used in business letters. **Open** punctuation has no punctuation mark after the salutation or complimentary close. **Mixed** punctuation contains a colon (:) after the salutation and a comma (,) after the complimentary close.

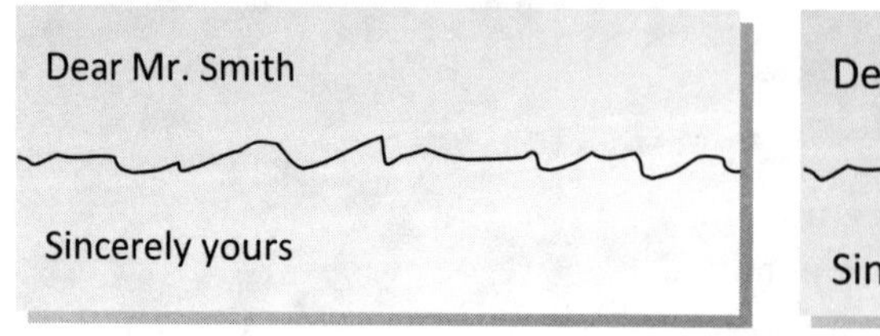

Open Punctuation   **Mixed Punctuation**

ADDITIONAL LETTER FEATURES

Some additional letter features that may be used are described below.

USPS letter address style. The letter address of a business or personal-business letter may be keyed in ALL CAPS with no punctuation if using the United States Postal Service style for the delivery (envelope) address.

Second-page heading. If a letter is longer than one page, a plain sheet of paper is used for the second and succeeding pages. Only the first page contains the sender's letterhead. A second-page heading should be keyed 1" from the top of the page in block format, SS. Include the name of the addressee, the word *Page* followed by the page number, and the date. DS below the date before continuing the letter.

TM 1"
Ms. Barbara Powell
Page 2
July 22, 20--
↓1
The remaining paragraphs of the letter will be keyed here.

Widow/Orphan. At least two lines of a paragraph must be keyed at the bottom of the first page of a letter and at the top of the second page. Activate the Widow/Orphan feature to ensure proper breaks.

Bullets and Numbering. Use the Bullets feature or Numbering feature to create bulleted or numbered lists. These features automatically format each listed item in hanging indent style (the second and succeeding lines align under the first letter of the first word).

- Basic letter parts are letterhead, date, letter address, salutation, body, complimentary close, writer's name, and reference initials.

- Business letter formats are block, modified block with paragraph indentation, and modi-fied block without paragraph indentation.

Note the alignment of the bulleted items.

Tables in letters. A table inserted in a letter should be placed even with the left and right margins of the letter or centered between the margins. Leave a blank line above and below the inserted table. Table gridlines may be shown or hidden.

Form letters. A form letter is a standard message sent to more than one addressee. Form paragraphs may be stored as macros (stored text) and played back when needed to create personalized form letters. Form letters can also be created using the Mail Merge feature of word processing programs.

At 2" (3 returns down)

Return address
230 Glendale Court
Brooklyn, NY 11234-3721
February 15, 20— ↓2

Letter mailing address
Ms. Julie Hutchinson
1825 Melbourne Avenue
Flushing, NY 11367-2351 ↓1

Salutation
Dear Julie ↓1

Body
It seems like years since we were in Ms. Gerhig's keyboarding class. Now I wish I had paid more attention. As I indicated on the phone, I am applying for a position as box office coordinator for one of the theatres on Broadway. Of course, I know the importance o having my letter of application and resume formatted correctly, but I'm not sure that I remember how to do it. ↓1

Since you just completed your business education degree, I knew where to get the help I needed. Thanks for agreeing to look over my application documents; they are enclosed. Also, if you have any suggestions for changes to the content, please share those with me too. This job is so important to me; it's the one I really want. ↓1

Thanks again for agreeing to help. If I get the job, I'll take you out to one of New York's finest restaurants. ↓1

Default or 1" SM

Complimentary close
Sincerely ↓2

Writer
Rebecca Dunworthy ↓1

Enclosure notation
Enclosure

> Hold down the Shift key when you return after the first two lines of the Return address and the first two lines of the Letter address to avoid having extra space between lines.

> Shown in 11-point Calibri with 2" top margin and 1" side margins, this letter appears smaller than actual size.

Personal-Business Letter in Block Format

Approximately 2" TM
or Center Vertically

Begin Dateline, Complimentary Close,
Writer's name and title at same tab at
or near the center.

Date   September 15, 20-- ↓1

Mailing   FACSIMILE ↓1
notation

Attention line in   Attention Training and Development Department ↓1   ⎫ Remove space after paragraph—
letter address   Science Technologies ↓1   ⎬ use Shift Enter to insert Line Break
                     3368 Bay Path Road ↓1   ⎭ after first three lines.
                     Miami, FL 33160-3368 ↓1

Salutation   Ladies and Gentlemen: ↓1

Subject line   MODIFIED BLOCK FORMAT ↓1

                 This letter is arranged in modified block format. In this letter format the date and closing lines (compli-
Body   mentary close, name of the writer, and the writer's title) begin at or near horizontalcenter. In block
                 format all letter parts begin at the left margin. ↓1

Default or 1.25" Mixed punctuation (a colon after the salutation and a comma after the complimentary close) is used in
LM and RM   this example. Open punctuation (no mark after the salutation or complimentary close)may be used
                  with the modified block format if you prefer. ↓1

                 The first line of each paragraph may be blocked as shown here or indented one-half inch. If paragraphs
                 are indented, the optional subject line may be indented or centered. If paragraphs are blocked at the
                 left margin, the subject line is blocked, too. ↓1

Complimentary   Sincerely, ↓2
close

Writer   Derek Alan ↓1   ⎫ Remove space after paragraph—
Writer's title   Manager ↓1   ⎬ use Shift Enter to insert Line Break
                                                                                    ⎭ after name.

Reference   DA:xx ↓1
initials

Enclosure   Enclosure ↓1
notation

Copy notation   c Kimberly Rodriquez-Duarte ↓1

Postscript   A block format letter is enclosed so that you can compare the two formats. As you can see,
                 either format presents an attractive appearance.

At least 1" BM

Letter in Modified Block Format

ENVELOPES

Most word processing programs have an Envelope feature that will automatically format the placement of the return and letter addresses. However, because of printer issues, not all users are able to use the Envelope feature efficiently. Therefore, specific keying instructions are provided below for formatting envelopes.

- **Sender's return address.** Key the return address in block style, SS, approximately 0.25" from the left and top margins of the envelope. Key the name, street address, city, state, and ZIP Code in three lines either in ALL CAPS or Initial Caps.

- **Receiver's address.** Key the receiver's address in block style, SS, and Initial Caps. You may use ALL CAPS if desired. Place the city, state, and ZIP Code (one space precedes the ZIP) on the last address line. Never abbreviate the name of a city or country.

- **International addresses.** Omit postal (ZIP) codes from the last line of addresses outside the U.S. Show only the name of the country on the last line, as shown below.

  > Mr. Hiram Sanders
  > 2121 Clearwater Street
  > Ottawa ON KIA OB1
  > CANADA

- **Spacing.** If not using the Envelope feature, tab over 2.5" for a small envelope (No. 6¾) and 4" for a large envelope (No. 10). Enter hard returns to place the first line of the delivery address approximately 2" from the top of the envelope.

- **Mailing and addressee notations.** Key a mailing notation (REGISTERED, SPECIAL DELIVERY) in ALL CAPS below the stamp, approximately ½" above the first line of the delivery address. Key an addressee notation (PERSONAL, CONFIDENTIAL) at the left margin a DS below the return address. If an attention line is used, key it as the first line of the delivery address.

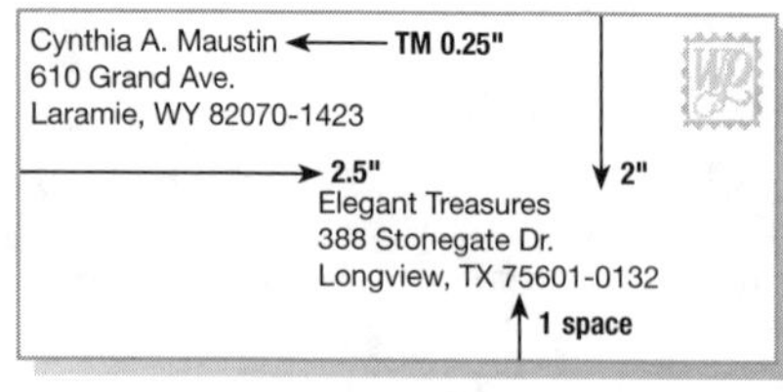

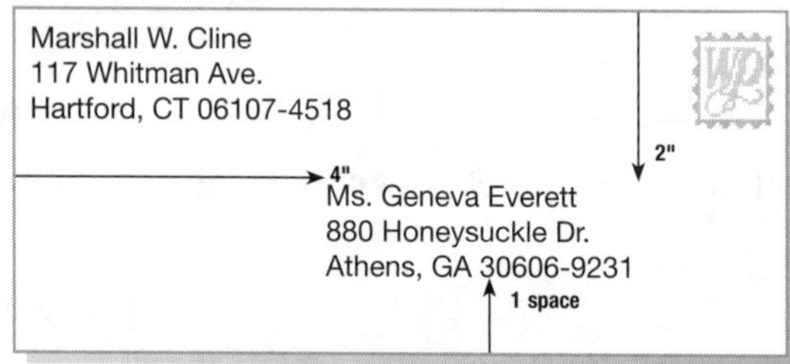

INTEROFFICE MEMOS

Interoffice memorandums (memos) are used by employees within an organization to communicate with one another. A memo heading consists of four standard parts: TO, FROM, DATE, and SUBJECT. (See p. 18 for an illustration of an interoffice memo.)

The memo is usually keyed on a preprinted form with the organization's name printed at the top of the page. If the headings TO, FROM, DATE, and SUBJECT need to be keyed, use the format guides presented below.

Memo margins.

Top margin	2"
Side margins	1" or default
Bottom margin	about 1"

Spacing. Begin all lines of the heading at the left margin. Leave one space above and below each part of the heading and below the subject. Use default tabs as shown below.

TO:	Tab twice to key recipient's name. ↓1
FROM:	Tab twice to key sender's name. ↓1
DATE:	Tab twice to key date. ↓1
SUBJECT:	Tab once to key subject. ↓1

Body. Begin all paragraphs of the memo at the left margin and key them SS with one blank line between paragraphs.

Reference initials. If someone other than the originator keys the memo, the keyboard operator's initials are keyed one line below the body of the memo.

In addition to the standard parts, an interoffice memo may include the following special parts.

Distribution list. When a memo is sent to more than one person, a distribution list is used. Format the TO heading as shown in the example below:

TO:	Kayla Breckenridge
	Paul Cooper
	Sandra Cox
	Michael Williams

Attachment/Enclosure notation. If another document is attached to a memo, the word *Attachment* is keyed at the left margin one line below the reference initials. If a document is included but not attached, the word *Enclosure* is used. If no reference initials are used, the notation is keyed one line below the last line of the body.

Copy notations. A copy notation indicates that a copy of the memo is being sent to someone besides the addressee. Key *c* followed by the name(s) of the person(s) who are to receive a copy. Place the copy notation one line below the enclosure notation or the reference initials.

Sometimes the writer of the memo wants to send a copy to someone without disclosing this to the addressee of the memo. In this case, key *bc* (blind copy) followed by the name(s). The blind copy notation is keyed only on the copy or copies, not on the original.

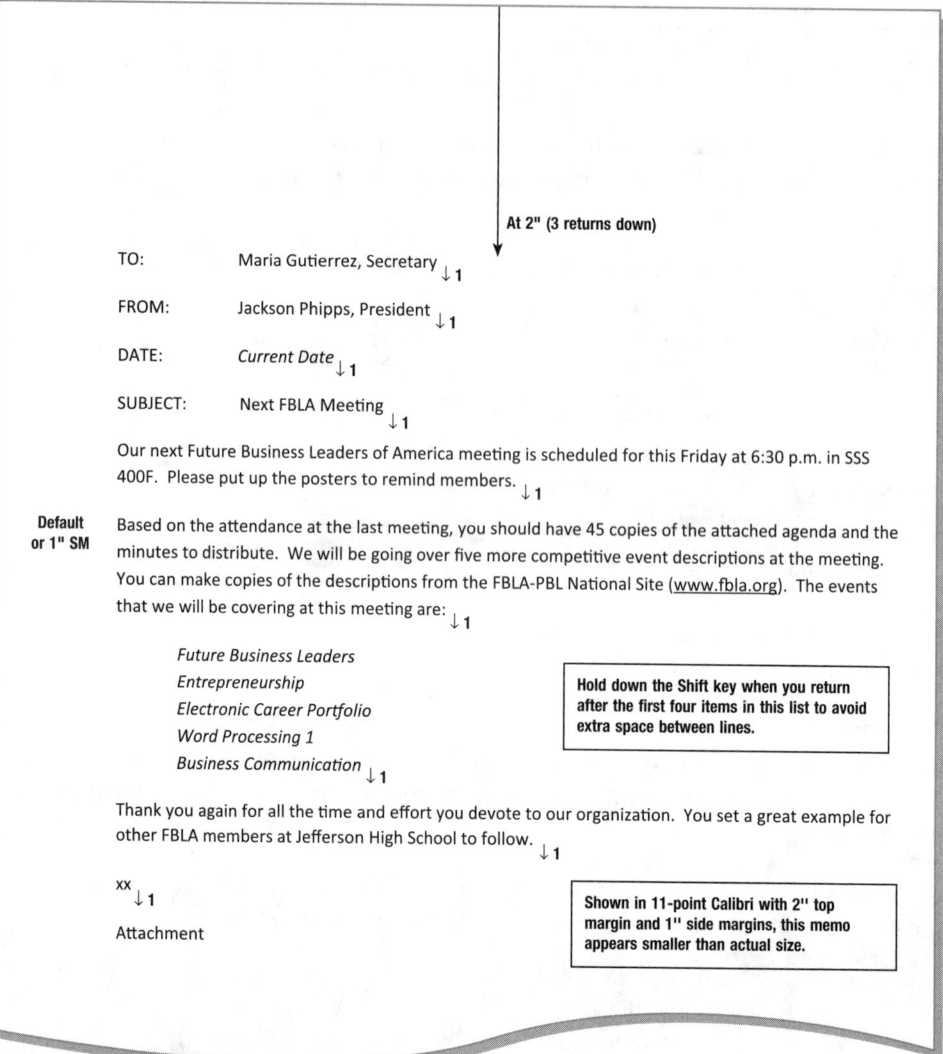

Interoffice Memo

E-MAIL

E-mail (electronic mail) is a popular way for businesspeople to communicate both inside and outside their organizations because of its speed in creating and sending messages. The delivery of e-mail can take place within minutes of its creation, whether the receiver is in the same building as the sender or thousands of miles away.

The format of an e-mail message is similar to an interoffice memo but may vary slightly depending upon the software that is used. See p. 20 for a model of a typical e-mail message.

E-mail headings. Most e-mail software includes *To, cc* (courtesy copy), and *Subject* headings on the originator (sender's) e-mail screen. Some also include a *bcc* (blind courtesy copy) line. The *Date* and *From* headings are automatically added when the e-mail is sent.

Body. The body of an e-mail message follows the same format as the interoffice memo. Key the paragraphs SS at the left margin with one line between paragraphs.

Special features of e-mail. Several additional features make e-mail's use even faster and more efficient. These features include the following.

- Maintaining an **e-mail address book** is a benefit when using e-mail. An address or addresses can be entered on the TO line by selecting the address book and clicking the name(s) of the receiver(s). This eliminates the job of keying each e-mail address.

- A **distribution or mailing list** can be created, allowing the sender to select only the group name when sending a multi-address e-mail. Members of a group can be added or deleted at any time. This feature saves time if e-mails are sent often to the same group of individuals.

- Files can be sent over the Internet as **attachments** to e-mail messages. Documents such as letters, reports, tables, and spreadsheets can be attached and sent electronically.

- Any message that is received can be **forwarded** to someone else. When a message is forwarded, a copy of the original message is sent to the new receiver without the knowledge of the original sender.

- The **Reply** feature is used to respond quickly to incoming e-mail. The incoming message (unless deleted) and reply are sent to the sender of the original message. The originator's address does not have to be keyed. The original message quickly reminds the originator what the reply is about, so a brief reply is sufficient.
  The **Reply All** feature, on some e-mail software, is used to respond to all copy recipients as well as the originator of an incoming message.

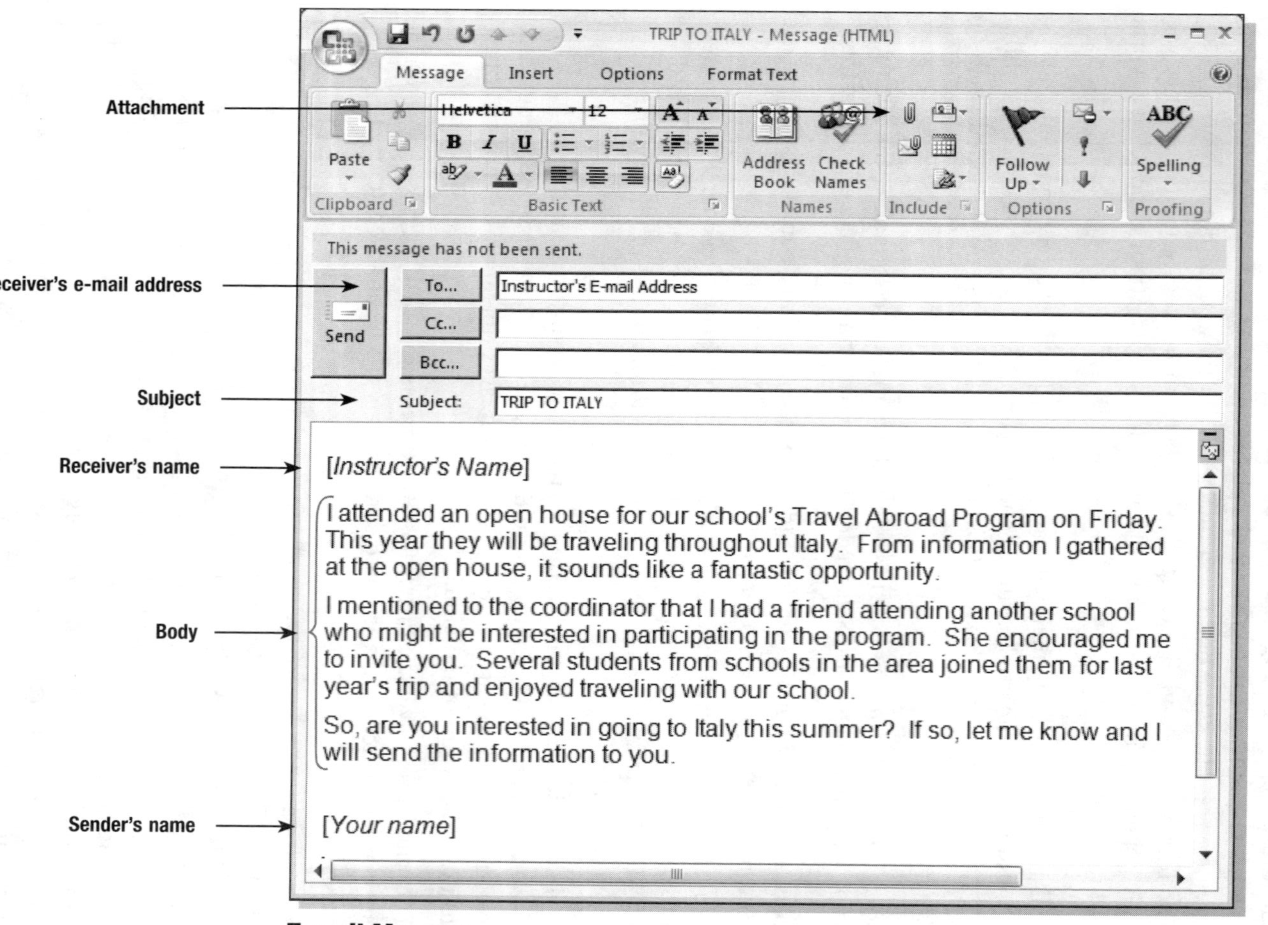

E-mail Message

REPORTS

A **report** is an account or summary of research findings, business proceedings, or some other topic that is written in an organized format.

Short (one- or two-page) reports are often prepared without covers or binders. Pages are usually fastened together in the upper-left corner by a staple or paper clip. Such reports are called **unbound reports**. See p. 30 for an illustration of an unbound report.

The following table shows the standard margins for unbound reports.

Side margins	1″
Top margin	2″ – First page 1″ – Second and succeeding pages
Bottom margin	At least 1″

Longer reports (three or more pages) are generally **bound** at the left margin. The binding takes about 0.5″ of space. To accommodate the binding, the left margin is increased to 1.5″ on all pages. Other standard margins in the above table apply to bound reports.

Word processing software automatically enters a soft page return when the bottom margin is reached. An exact 1″ bottom margin is not always possible; it may be adjusted to prevent a side heading or first line of a paragraph from printing as the last line of a page (orphan), or the last line of a paragraph from occurring at the top of a new page (widow). The Widow/Orphan feature automatically adjusts the bottom margin to accommodate these rules.

HEADINGS

Three types of headings are commonly used in reports:

- **Main heading (report title).** Center the main heading in the Title style. The default Title style is 26-point Cambria with a bottom border.

- **Side headings.** Begin side headings at the left margin. Capitalize the first letter of the first word and all other main words in each heading. Use Heading 1 style. The default Heading 1 style is 14-point Cambria.

- **Paragraph headings.** Paragraph headings are keyed at the left margin in 11-point Cambria and are bolded and italicized. Capitalize only the first letter of the first word and any proper nouns. Place a period after the heading.

Main Heading

Side Heading

Paragraph heading. The text begins on the same line.

SPACING

Refer to the model bound report on p. 32. All parts of the report are SS using the 1.15 default line spacing.

PAGE NUMBERING

The first page of a report usually is not numbered. If a page number is used on the first page, position it at the bottom of the page using center alignment. On the second and subsequent pages, position the page number at the top-right margin.

TITLE PAGE

A title page, or cover, is usually prepared for a bound report. To format a title page:

- Center and bold the title in ALL CAPS, bold and 14-point, 2" from the top of the page.
- Center the writer's name in capital and lowercase letters 5" from the top. Use 11-point type.
- Center the school name (or other organization) a DS below the writer's name.
- Center the date approximately 9" from the top of the page.

  See the illustration of a bound title page on p. 31.

TABLE OF CONTENTS

A table of contents lists the side and paragraph headings of a report and the page numbers where those headings can be found in the body. To format a table of contents:

- Use the same side and top margins that were used in the report.
- Key the heading Table of Contents in Title style, 2" from the top of the paper. DS below the heading.

- Begin side headings at the left margin.

- Indent paragraph headings 0.5".

- Insert dot leaders to lead the reader's eye from the headings to the page numbers.

See the illustration of a table of contents on p. 31.

NUMBERED AND BULLETED LISTS

Number items or paragraphs to show the proper order of a series of steps. Use bullets in a list to add emphasis to text.

- Indent numbered items 0.25" from the left margin; block the lines at that point as shown in the following example. If the Numbering feature is used, enumerated items are automatically indented correctly.

> 1. Establish and maintain eye contact with your audience.
> 2. Speak clearly, distinctly, and slowly. Make sure you speak loudly enough that everyone in the room can hear you.

- Leave a blank line above and below a numbered or bulleted list.

INSERTED TABLES

Insert a table as near as possible to the text that it illustrates. Format the table as follows:

- Leave a blank line above and below the table.

- Center the main heading (identification) above the table or in Row 1.

- Center the table horizontally within the left and right margins.

- Gridlines may be shown or hidden.

DOCUMENTATION

Documentation refers to providing proof that information contained in a report is accurate. Citing published material—books, magazine articles, pamphlets, Web sites, etc.—of numerous authors adds credibility to the report. Credit must be given for citations of both **direct quotations** (someone else's actual words) and **paraphrased** words (someone else's idea stated in the report writer's words).

Quotations of up to three keyed lines are enclosed in quotation marks in the body of the report. See p. 30. Long quotations (four lines or more) should be indented 0.5" from the left margin. See p. 32. (Long quotations may be left *and* right indented 0.5".) Paraphrased material is not enclosed in quotation marks, nor is it indented.

An **ellipsis** (. . .) is used to indicate material omitted from a quotation. An ellipsis is three periods, each preceded and followed by a space. If the omitted material occurs at the end of a sentence, include the period or other punctuation before the ellipsis, as shown below.

Methods of referencing cited material in the body of reports include textual citations, footnotes, and endnotes.

Textual citations. Textual citations are generally keyed in parentheses in the report body immediately following the quoted material. Textual citations include the name(s) of the author(s), year of publication, and page number(s) of the reference material. The words *year* and *page* are not included. See example below.

> Nothing can engage an audience more quickly, or make a point more effectively, than a well-chosen illustration . . . (Brown, 2009, 28).

When the author's name is used in the text introducing the quotation, only the year of publication and the page number(s) appear in parentheses.

> J. Blackburn (2009, 426) stated that. . . .

When no author is listed for a work, cite the title of the work and the year published. Use quotation marks around the title of an article or chapter and italicize the title of a periodical or book.

Footnotes. The footnote method of documentation identifies the reference cited by a superscript number. (The superscript number is inserted automatically if the Footnote and Endnote feature is used to insert footnotes.)

The complete documentation for the reference is placed at the bottom of the same page and is identified with the same superscript number. The first line of each footnote is indented 0.5". Footnotes are keyed SS, with a DS between them. (If paragraphs are SS and blocked, footnotes are not indented.) Footnotes should be numbered consecutively throughout the report. See the footnotes illustrated on p. 32.

Endnotes. The endnote method of documentation also identifies the reference cited by a superscript number. However, the complete documentation for the reference is placed on a separate page at the end of the report in a section titled Endnotes. To format an endnotes page:

- Identify each endnote with a corresponding superscript number. (The Footnote and Endnote feature automatically inserts a superscript number).
- Use the same top and side margins as the first page of the report.
- Center the heading Endnotes.
- Insert a page number at the top right margin.

■ SS each endnote, and DS between endnotes.

■ Indent the first line of each endnote 0.5" from the left margin; all other lines begin at the left margin.

Century 21 **style.** When keying footnotes and endnotes, follow the conventions for formatting names, titles, dates, etc. The examples shown below illustrate the *Century 21* footnote/endnote style.

For a Book:

[1]Author(s)' First and Last Name(s), *Book Title* (City of Publication: Publishing Company, Year of Publication), p. #.

Examples:

[1]Robert K. Schaeffer, *Understanding Globalization,* (Lanham, MD: Rowman & Littlefield Publishers, Inc., 2007), p. 1.

[1]Nancy Prince and Jeanie Jackson, *Exploring Theater* (Minneapolis/St. Paul: West Publishing Company, 2007), p. 35.

[1]Robert Gerver, et al., *South-Western Geometry: An Integrated Approach* (Cincinnati: South-Western, Cengage Learning, 2008), p. 637.

Note: If the book reference contains more than three authors, key *et al.* following the name of the first author listed: Robert Gerver, et al., . . .

For a Journal or Magazine Article:

[2]Author(s)' First and Last Name(s), "Article Title," *Magazine Title* (Publication Date), p. #.

Example:

[2]Richard G. Harris, "Globalization, Trade, and Income," *Canadian Journal of Economics*, November 2003), p. 755.

For an Encyclopedia or Reference Book:

[3]*Reference Book*, Vol. # (City of Publication: Publishing Company, Year of Publication), p. #.

Example:

[3]*Encyclopedia Americana*, Vol. 25 (Danbury, CT: Grolier Incorporated, 2008), p. 637.

For a Web Site:

[4]Author(s)' First and Last Name(s) (if given), "Article Title," Web Address, (Month Day, Year).

Note: Show the date the site was posted; if not given, show the date of online visit.

Example:

> [4]Stephen Railton, "Your Mark Twain," http://www.etext.lib.virginia.edu/railton/sc_as_mt/yourmt13.html, (24 September, 1999).

For an Online Journal, Magazine, or Newspaper:

[5]Author(s)' First and Last Name(s) (if given), "Article Title," *Magazine Title,* Publication Date, Web Address, Month Day, Year.

Example:

> [5]John E. Lee, "Technology Aids in Stopping Copyright Offenders," *Hopper Business Journal*, Fall 2006, http//www.hpj.edu/technologyaids.htm, December 26, 2008.

For an E-mail:

[6]Sender(s)' First and Last Name(s), Sender(s)' E-mail Address. "Subject of E-mail." E-mail to Receiver(s)' First and Last Name(s), Receiver(s)' E-Mail Address(es), Month Day, Year.

REFERENCES PAGE

Each type of documentation (textual citation, footnotes, and endnotes) requires a references page. All references cited in the report are listed on a separate page under the heading References or Works Cited. Short unbound reports can list references on the last page of the report. See the illustration on p. 30.

Use the heading Bibliography if related materials were also used. This heading will encompass all material that was referenced, as well as material used but not cited.

Format the references page as follows:

- Use the same margins as the first page of the report.

- Include a page number at the top right.

- Center the heading References in Title style.

- DS between the heading and the first reference. SS each reference; DS between references.

- List all references alphabetically by authors' last names. If there is no author, the title moves to the author position, and the entry is alphabetized by the first significant word of the title.

- Begin the first line of each reference at the left margin; indent additional lines 0.5" (hanging indent style).

Note that on the references page, the references are keyed in a different format than that used for footnotes and endnotes. See the examples below.

For a Book:

Schaeffer, Robert K. *Understanding Globalization.* (Lanham, MD: Rowman & Littlefield Publishers, Inc., 2007).

Prince, Nancy, and Jeanie Jackson. *Exploring Theater.* Minneapolis/St. Paul: West Publishing Company, 2009.

Gerver, Robert, et al. *South-Western Geometry: An Integrated Approach.* Cincinnati: South-Western, Cengage Learning, 2008.

For a Journal or Magazine Article:

Harris, Richard G. "Globalization, Trade, and Income." *Canadian Journal of Economics,* November 1993, 755–776.

For an Encyclopedia or Reference Book:

Encyclopedia Americana, Vol. 25. "Statue of Liberty." Danbury, CT: Grolier Incorporated, 2009.

For a Web Site:

Railton, Stephen. "Your Mark Twain." http://www.etext.lib.virginia.edu/railton/sc_as_mt/yourmt13.html (24 September, 1999).

For an Online Journal, Magazine, or Newspaper:

Lee, John E. "Technology Aids in Stopping Copyright Offenders." *Hopper Business Journal,* (Fall 2000). http//www.hpj.edu/technologyaids.htm (December 26, 2008).

For an E-mail:

Devaul, Payton. pdevaul@mail.com. "Basketball Scholarship." E-mail to Kirk Stennis, kstennis@umt.edu. April 15, 2006.

MODERN LANGUAGE ASSOCIATION (MLA) REPORT STYLE

The Modern Language Association (MLA) style is often used to format and document school reports. The MLA documentation method, also called *parenthetical reference*, is similar to *Century 21*'s textual citation method. The MLA report style has these distinctive format features (illustrated on p. 33):

Margins. On all pages, the top, bottom, left, and right margins are 1".

Header and page number. The header contains the page number, right-aligned. Every page is numbered, including the first. The writer's last name precedes the page number.

Line spacing. The entire report is DS, including long quotations, bulleted and numbered items, report identification, tables, and works cited. Before you begin to key, set Line Spacing to 2.0 with 0 points of spacing after paragraphs.

Report identification. The writer's name, instructor's name, course title, and date (day/month/year style) are keyed DS on separate lines at the top left margin on the first page.

Report title. The title is centered a DS below the date in title case. The body begins a DS below the title.

Indentations and long quotations. The first line of each paragraph is indented 0.5". Long quotations (four or more lines) are indented 1" (or at the second default tab setting) from the left margin and DS.

Inserted tables. A table should be inserted as near as possible to the text that it illustrates. Format the table as follows:

- Key a number (*Table 1*) and caption (title) above the table, left-aligned.
- DS above the table number, below the last line (or source note) of the table, and between lines within the table.
- Hide table gridlines and adjust the table width to fit within the left and right margins.

References page. Format the MLA reference page as follows: (See the Works Cited page illustrated on p. 33.)

- Use 1" margins.
- Center the heading **Works Cited** at the top margin.
- DS below the heading.
- List all references in alphabetical order by authors' last name.

- DS all entries as well as between entries.

- Begin the first line of each reference at the left margin; indent other lines 0.5" (hanging indent style).

Binding. Staple or clip all pages of the report at the top left corner.

RELATED DOCUMENTS

Many business documents may be keyed in unbound or bound report format. Two such documents are the news release and summary meeting minutes. A **news release** is a document used by a company to make a public announcement. **Summary meeting minutes** are the official record of what was said and done at a meeting. See illustrations on p. 34.

News release. Use the format guides for unbound reports except:

- Key the heading **News Release** at the top left margin in Title style.

- On the next line at the left margin, key **For Release:** in Subtitle style. Below it, key **Contact:** in Subtitle style at the left margin. Tap ENTER once; begin the news release body.

- Key the news release body in 1.15 line spacing.

- Center the symbols ### below the last line.

Summary meeting minutes. Use the format guides for unbound reports except:

- Use 1.15 line spacing with 10-point spacing after paragraphs.

- Number each item of business summarized in the minutes. The Numbered List feature may be used.

2" TM

Title

Samuel Clemens ("Mark Twain")

Report body

Samuel Clemens was one of America's most renowned authors. The colorful life he led was the basis for his writing. Although his formal education ended when he was 12 years old with the death of his father, his varied career interests provided an informal education, not unlike many others of his generation. Clemens brings these rich experiences to life in his writing.

Textual citation

Sam Clemens was recognized for his fiction as well as for his humor. It has been said that " . . . next to sunshine and fresh air Mark Twain's humor has done more for the welfare of mankind than any other agency" (Railton, "Your Mark Twain," 2003). By cleverly weaving fiction and humor, he developed many literary masterpieces. Some say his greatest masterpiece was "Mark Twain," a pen name (pseudonym)

Textual citation

Clemens first used in the Nevada Territory in 1863. This fictitious name became a kind of mythic hero to the American public (Railton, "Sam Clemens as Mark Twain," 2003).

1" SM

Mark Twain was brought to national prominence when his first book, *The Celebrated Jumping Frog of Calaveras County and other Sketches*, was published in 1867. The book was comprised of 27 sketches, some of which had previously been published in newspapers. Some of his masterpieces that are among his most widely read books are *The Adventures of Tom Sawyer*, *Adventures of Huckleberry Finn*, and *The Prince and the Pauper*.

Side heading

The Adventures of Tom Sawyer

The Adventures of Tom Sawyer was first published in 1876. Such characters as Tom Sawyer, Aunt Polly, Becky Thatcher, and Huck Finn have captured the attention of readers for generations. Boys and girls, young and old, enjoy Tom Sawyer's mischievousness. Who can forget how Tom shared the privilege of whitewashing Aunt Polly's fence? What child isn't fascinated by the episode of Tom and Becky lost in the cave?

Side heading

Adventures of Huckleberry Finn

Adventures of Huckleberry Finn, the story about a boy who runs away from home and lives in the wild, has appealed to young and old alike since it was first published in 1885. Many of the characters included in *The Adventures of Tom Sawyer* surface again in *Huckleberry Finn*. The widow Douglas and the widow's sister, Miss Watson, provide formidable foes for Huckleberry despite their good intentions.

Children are able to live vicariously through Huck. What child hasn't dreamed of sneaking out of the house at night and running away to live a lifestyle of their own making?

About
1" BM

Unbound Report with Textual Citations

Title

References

Railton, Stephen. "Your Mark Twain." http://etext.lib.virginia.edu/railton/sc_as_mt/yourmt13.html (accessed October 23, 2007).

List of references

Railton, Stephen. "Sam Clemens as Mark Twain." http://etext.virginia.edu/railton/sc_as_mt/cathompg.html (accessed October 14, 2007).

Waisman, Michael. "About Mark Twain." http://www.geocities.com/swaisman/huckfinn.htm (accessed October 18, 2007).

References Page

Delivering the Mail

Name of Student

20--

**Bound Report
Title Page**

Table of Contents

**Table of
Contents**

Delivering the Mail

For years, people have used written communication as one of their primary means of exchanging information. Those using this form of communicating have depended on the U.S. mail to transport their messages from one place to another.

> For much of American history, the mail was our main form of organized communication. Americans wanting to know the state of the world, the health of a friend, or the fate of their business anxiously awaited the mail. To advise a distant relative, to order goods, to pay a bill, to express views to their congressman or love to their fiancée, they used the mail. No American institution has been more intimately involved in daily hopes and fears.[i]

The history of the U.S. mail is not only interesting but also reflective of the changes in American society, specifically transportation. A variety of modes of transporting mail have been used over the years. Speed, of course, was the driving force behind most of the changes.

Steamboats

Congress used inventions to move the mail from place to place. In 1813, five years after Robert Fulton's first experiments on the Hudson River, Congress authorized the Post Office to transport mail by steamboat.[ii] Transporting mail to river cities worked very well. However, the efficiency of using steamboats to transport mail between New York and San Francisco was questionable. "The distance was 19,000 miles and the trip could take as long as six to seven months.[iii]

Railroads

Although mail was carried by railr
railroads to be post roads.[iv] Train
decreased substantially, making it

No aspect of American life was un
service almost to the level of a fre
called for an increase in the cost o
for two cents.)[v]

**Bound Report
with Long
Quotations,
Endnotes**

2" TM

Title # Globalization

Footnote
Superscript
We live in a time of worldwide change. What happens in one part of the world impacts people on the other side of the world. People around the world are influenced by common developments.[1]

The term "globalization" is used to describe this phenomenon. According to Harris, the term is being used in a variety of contexts.[2] However, in the broadest context globalization can be defined as:

Long
Quote
> . . . a process of interaction and integration among the people, companies, and governments of different nations, a process driven by international trade and investment and aided by information technology. This process has effects on the environment, on culture, on political systems, on economic development and prosperity, and on human physical well-being in societies around the world.[3]

1.5" LM

1.0" RM

The business world uses this term in a narrower context to refer to the production, distribution, and marketing of goods and services at an international level. Everyone is impacted by the continued increase of globalization in a variety of ways. The types of food we eat, the kinds of clothes we wear, the variety of technologies we utilize, the modes of transportation available to us, and the types of jobs we pursue are directly linked to globalization. Globalization is changing the world we live in.

Side Heading ### Causes of Globalization

Harris indicates that there are three main factors contributing to globalization. These factors include:

Footnotes
[1] Robert K. Schaeffer, *Understanding Globalization* (Lanham, MD: Rowman & Littlefield Publishers, Inc., 1977), p. 1.

[2] Richard G. Harris, "Globalization, Trade, and Income," *Canadian Journal of Economics*, November 1993, p. 755.

[3] "Globalization 101.org," http://www.globalization101.org/What_is_Globalization.html (accessed November 1, 2007).

**Bound Report
with Footnotes**

Use Line Spacing 2.0 for
all lines in a MLA Report

1" TM

Henderson 1   **Header**

DS I.D.
Information

James Henderson

Professor Lewis

HC101 Composition

15 February 20--

Career Planning

Indent ¶ 0.5"
and DS ¶s

Career planning is an important, ongoing process. It is important because the career you choose

will affect your quality of life.

One important step in career planning is to define your career goals.

Indent long
quotes 1" from
LM and DS

Whatever your present plans for employment or further education, you should

consider your long-term career goals. You might wonder why someone who is

considering a first job should be thinking beyond that job. Thinking ahead may

help you choose a first job that is closely related to long-term interests. . . . With a

career goal in mind, you can evaluate beginning job offers in relation to that goal.

1" LM and RM

(Oliverio, Pasewark, and White 516)

1" LM and RM

Another useful step in career planning is to develop a personal profile of your skills, interests, and

values.

An analysis of your skills is likely to reveal that you have many different kinds: (1) functional

skills that determine how well you manage time, communicate, and motivate people; (2) adaptive skills

that determine your efficiency, flexibility, reliability, and enthusiasm; and (3) technical skills such as

keyboarding, computer, and language skills that are required for many jobs.

Values are "principles that guide a person's life" (Fulton-Calkins and Stulz 543), and you should

identify them early so that you can pursue a career that will improve your chances to acquire them.

Values include the importance you place on family, security, wealth, prestige, creativity, power, and

independence.

At least 1" BM

**MLA Report,
page 1**

1" TM

Henderson 2   Header

Interests are best described as activities you like and enthusiastically pursue. By listing and

analyzing your interests, you should be able to identify a desirable work environment. For example, your

list is likely to reveal if you like to work with things or people, work alone or with others, lead or follow

others, or be indoors or outdoors.

**MLA Report,
page 2**

1" TM

Henderson 3   Header

Works Cited

Fulton-Calkins, Patsy and Karin M. Stulz. *Procedures & Theory for Administrative*

Hanging indent
with 0.5"
indentation

Professionals. 5th ed. Cincinnati: South-Western, 2004.

Oliverio, Mary Ellen, William R. Pasewark, and Bonnie R. White. *The Office: Procedures and*

Technology. 4th ed. Cincinnati: South-Western, 2003.

**Works
Cited
Page**

News Release

For Release: Immediate
Contact: Heidi Zemack

CLEVELAND, OH, May 25, 20--. Science teachers from school districts in six counties are eligible for this year's Teacher Excellence awards funded by The Society for Environmental Engineers.

Nominations can be submitted through Friday, July 31, by students, parents, residents, and other educators. Nomination forms are available from the participating school districts or on the Society's website at http://www.tsee.webhost.com.

An anonymous committee reviews the nominations and selects ten finalists. From that group, seven "teachers of distinction" and three award winners are selected. The top award winner receives $5,000, the second receives $2,500, and the third receives $1,500. Each teacher of distinction receives $500. The teachers of distinction and the award winners will be announced on September 5 at a dinner at the Cleveland Inn.

School districts participating in the program include those in these counties: Cuyahoga, Lorain, Medina, Summit, Lake, and Geauga.

News Release

WOODWARD HIGH SCHOOL BIOLOGY CLUB

Meeting Minutes

March 2, 20--

1. Call to order: President Marcie Holmquist called the Biology Club meeting to order at 2:45 p.m. on March 2, 20-- in Room 214.

2. Attendance: Jerry Finley, Secretary, recorded the attendance. All officers, 23 members, and the faculty sponsor were present.

3. Approval of minutes: The minutes were approved as read by Jerry Finley.

4. This unfinished business was acted upon:

   a. There will be five teams of four members each for the candy sale that begins on May 1. Team captains are Bruce Holstein, Anita Jones, Roberto Nuez, Ty Billops, and Gracie Walton. Each captain will select three members for his/her team.

   b. Bill Eaton will organize a team of volunteers for the Route 163 project. He will try to get at least 15 members to clean up the litter on May 15. The Chamber of Commerce will provide adult supervision, safety vests and gloves, road signs, and collection bags. The volunteers will begin at 9:15 a.m. and work until about 11:30 a.m. They are to meet at the Carriage Inn parking lot at 8:45 a.m.

   c. The officers recommended that the Club not provide financial support for an international student this coming year since all members who attend the Fall Regional Leadership Conference will need financial assistance for travel, food, and lodging. The officers' recommendation was approved.

5. This new business was discussed and acted upon:

   a. President Holmquist appointed the Nominating Committee (Sissy Erwin, Roberta Shaw, and Jim Vance), and they are to present a slate of officers at the April meeting.

   b. The membership approved officers to attend the Spring Regional Leadership Conference at Great Valley Resort and Conference Center on April 12. Their expenses for travel and meals will be reimbursed.

6. The next meeting is April 3 at 2:45 p.m. in Room 103. The meeting was adjourned at 3:35 p.m. by Marcie Holmquist.

Minutes submitted by Jerry Finley, Secretary

Summary Meeting Minutes

TABLES

Tables are used extensively in business documents to organize and present information in a concise, logical manner. Tables consist of vertical columns and horizontal rows. The intersection of a column and row is called a **cell**.

When text is keyed in a cell, it wraps around in that cell instead of wrapping to the next row or column. A line space is added to the cell each time the text wraps. Use the TAB key or Right arrow key to move from column to column and from row to row. To move around in a filled-in table, use arrow keys, TAB, or the mouse (click the desired cell).

BASIC PARTS OF A TABLE

A table consists of several basic parts. (These parts are illustrated in the table on p. 38.)

1. **Main title** usually keyed in ALL CAPS, centered in the first row or placed above the table

2. **Secondary title** in capital and lowercase letters centered a DS below the main title

3. **Column headings** centered over the columns

4. **Body** consisting of the data entries

5. **Source note** keyed at the bottom left of the table

6. **Gridlines** on screen may be shown or hidden on printout

Note: If gridlines are hidden (not printed), column headings and the last entry in an amount column with a total should be underlined.

FORMATTING FEATURES

Most word processing programs have a Table feature for formatting tables. The following formatting features will produce a table that is attractive and easy to read.

- **Insert Table.** Use this feature to quickly specify the number of columns and rows in a new table.

- **AutoFormat.** Most word processing software has many pre-designed table formats from which to select. Because these designs include alignment, borders, effects, shading, and font, they save time. These formats can be modified for specific rows or columns or the entire table.

- **Bold, italic, and underline.** These font styles can be added prior to keying the text into the table or after the text has been entered. Use these elements sparingly for emphasis.

- **Borders.** Use the Borders feature to highlight important data. Borders can be added around an entire table or around selected cells, rows, or columns within a table. The color of table borders can be changed. One color may be used for all borders, or a different color may be used to highlight a specific cell, column, or row.

- **Column width.** In a newly created table, all columns are the same width. Column widths can be changed to accommodate entries of unequal widths. Generally, each column should be only slightly wider than the longest data entry in the column. Table columns should be identical widths or markedly different widths. Columns that are only slightly different widths should be avoided.

- **Delete/Insert rows and/or columns.** Delete empty rows or columns wherever they occur. Row(s) can be inserted as needed above or below an existing row. Column(s) can be inserted to the left or right of an existing column as needed.

- **Font color.** The Font Color feature changes text from black to one of many other colors. Use a font color that contrasts clearly with the background (shading or paper color). **Note:** The word processing features change border and font colors onscreen, but the printer must support color options for these changes to appear in printed documents.

- **Horizontal alignment.** Within columns, words may be left-aligned or center-aligned. Whole numbers are right-aligned if a column total is shown; decimal numbers are decimal-aligned. Other figures may be center-aligned.

- **Horizontal placement.** A table is most attractive when centered horizontally. The left and right margins will be equal.

- **Join/Split cells.** Join two or more cells into one cell for the main title, source note, and other data as needed. Use the Split feature to divide an existing cell into two or more smaller cells, if necessary.

- **Row height.** All rows, including title rows, may be the same height. To enhance the appearance and make the data easier to read, the row height can be adjusted to add more white space around the data. For example, the main title row may be slightly deeper than the secondary title row. The column heading row height may be less than the secondary title row but more than the data entry rows. See the table illustration below for varied row heights.

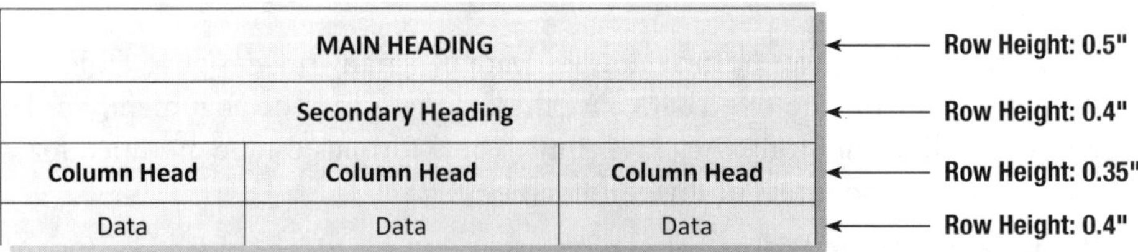

- **Shading.** The Shading feature can be used to highlight important information. Shading fills the selected area with varying shades of gray or color. The selected area may be the entire table or a single cell, column, or row within a table.

- **Sort.** The Sort feature arranges data entries in a specific order. In a table column, text can be sorted alphabetically in ascending (A to Z) or descending (Z to A) order. Also, numbers and dates can be sorted numerically (chronologically), in either ascending or descending order.

- **Tab stops and indentations.** Tab stops and indentations can be set within table cells in much the same way they are set in paragraphs. While all tab stops and indentations can be used within cells, the left tab, decimal tab, dot leader tabs, first-line indentation, and hanging indentation are used most frequently.

- **Vertical alignment.** Within cells, data may be aligned at the top, center, or bottom. Heading rows most often use center alignment. Data rows usually are either center- or bottom-aligned.

- **Vertical placement.** A table may be centered vertically (equal top and bottom margins), or it may begin 2" from the top edge of the page.

RELATED DOCUMENTS

Itineraries and agendas may be created using the Table feature. An **itinerary** is an outline of a person's travel activities for a specific period of time. An **agenda** is a list of things to be done or actions to be taken, usually at a meeting.

Itinerary. The information on an itinerary is attractively formatted to show at a glance the traveler's approximate location and activity at all times while away. An itinerary can be prepared as a centered table with or without gridlines. See the illustration on p. 39.

Agenda. An agenda contains two columns of text, connected by dot leaders. The document may be keyed within a two-column table (with gridlines hidden) or using tabs, as shown on p. 40.

For an agenda not keyed as a table, follow these format guides:

- 2" top margin on the first page or centered vertically

- 1" side margins and 1" bottom margin

- 1" top margin on second and succeeding pages

- DS main and secondary headings.

- DS above and below each main item; other items may be SS.

- Set a right dot leader tab at the right margin for text in the right column.

Vertical Centering
(equal top and
bottom margins)

Main heading

Secondary heading

Column headings

Body

Horizontal Centering (equal side margins)

BROADWAY GROSSES		
Week Ending 7/22/2007		
Production	*Gross This Week*	*Gross Last Week*
Wicked	$1,472,649	$1,468,400
The Lion King	1,283,279	1,291,898
Mary Poppins	1,226,944	1,191,101
Jersey Boys	1,197,014	1,211,053
Beauty and the Beast	1,139,499	1,095,124
Legally Blonde	946,840	939,285
Mamma Mia!	935,608	940,187
The Color Purple	926,764	974,904
Hairspray	865,744	809,462
Curtains	837,138	821,457
Totals	$10,831,479	$10,742,871

Source

Source: http://www.broadwayworld.com/grosses.cfm (24 July 2007).

Three-Column Table with Source Note

TRAVEL ITINERARY FOR LISA PEROTTA
222 Pine View Drive
Coraopolis, PA 15108
(412) 555-1320
perotta@fastnet.com
Pittsburgh, PA to Santa Ana, CA—April 18-22, 20--

Date	Time	Activity	Comments
Tuesday April 18	3:30 p.m. (ET)	Depart **Pittsburgh International Airport** (PIT) for Santa Ana, CA Airport (SNA) on **USEast Flight 146**. *Arrival time is 5:01 p.m.(PT)*	The flight is non-stop on an Airbus A319, and you are assigned seat 22E.
	5:30 p.m. (PT)	Reservation with **Star Car Rental** (714-555-0190). Return by 12 noon (PT) on April 22.	Confirmation No.: 33-345. Telephone: (714) 555-1030.
	6:00 p.m. (PT)	Reservations at the Hannah Hotel, 421 Race Avenue, Santa Ana for April 18 to April 22 for a single, non-smoking room at $145 plus tax. Telephone: (714)-490-1200.	Confirmation No: 632A-04/18. Check-in after 6 p.m. is guaranteed. Check out by 11 a.m.
Saturday April 22	1:25 p.m. (PT)	Depart **Santa Ana Airport** (SNA) for Pittsburgh International Airport (PIT) on **USEast Flight 148**. *Arrival time is 8:52 p.m. (ET).*	The flight is non-stop on an Airbus A319, and you are assigned seat 16A.
Travel Agency Contact Information—Agent is Mary Grecco; 444 Grant Street, Pittsburgh, PA 15219; Telephone: (412) 734-6687; Fax: (412) 734-6688; E-Mail: greccom@netway.com			

Itinerary

WOODWARD HIGH SCHOOL BIOLOGY CLUB

Agenda

March 2, 20--

2:45 p.m. in Room 214

Type of Meeting: Regular meeting

Meeting Facilitator: Marcie Holmquist, President

Invitees: All members and faculty sponsor

1) Call to order

2) Roll call

3) Approval of minutes from last meeting

4) Unfinished business

    a) Finalize team assignments for candy sale that begins May 1

    b) Plan approved community service project to care for one mile of State Route 163

    c) Discuss recommendation that the Club help support an international student

5) New business

    a) Appoint nominating committee

    b) Discuss plans for regional leadership conference on April 12

    c) Discuss annual give-back gift to Woodward High

6) Adjournment

Agenda

EMPLOYMENT DOCUMENTS

This section describes the contents of employment documents and provides format guides for them. As a prospective employee, you must prepare these documents carefully, providing accurate, error-free information.

RESUME (DATA SHEET)

Preparation for an employment interview begins with the preparation of a resume or data sheet. See pp. 43–44 for illustrations of a printed resume and an electronic resume.

A resume should include the following types of information:

- **Personal information.** Include your name, home address, e-mail address, and telephone number(s).

- **Objective.** Provide a clear definition of the position desired.

- **Education.** Include the school(s), graduation date(s), major or program completed, and grade point average. List skills acquired and relevant courses taken. Include grades earned in courses directly related to job competence.

- **School and/or community activities or accomplishments.** Include organizations, leadership positions, honors, and awards.

- **Work experience.** For each job held, provide the name and address of the organization/employer, applicant's position, and a brief description of responsibilities. Begin each descriptive sentence with an active verb, such as *served, assisted,* and *supervised.* The most current position is listed first in this section.

- **References.** Prepare a reference list with names, addresses, telephone numbers, and e-mail addresses to take to an employment interview. Select three to six people (not relatives) who are familiar with your job skills, work habits, personality, and character; obtain their approval in advance. If you prepare this list as a separate document, add the statement *"References will be furnished upon request"* to your resume. If preferred, the list of references may be added at the end of the resume.

Apply these guidelines to format a resume:

- **Use a simple format.** Top, bottom, and side margins of 1" are acceptable. You may use margins slightly less than 1" in order to fit the resume on one page.

- **Present the most important information first.** Recently graduated applicants should list educational background before work experience.

- **Key your name at the top of the page on a line by itself.** Key your address (standard, not USPS style) below your name, and list each telephone number on a separate line.

- **Arrange resume parts attractively on the page.** The arrangement may vary with personal preference and the purpose of the resume. Some large organizations offer a Web page on which job applicants can post electronic resumes. A printed resume can contain format features and enhancements such as bold, bullets, lines, borders, indentations, and columns. These features and enhancements may disappear partially or entirely when scanned, attached to e-mail, or posted to a Web page. Therefore, omit these elements on an electronic resume.

- **Use a basic font**, such as Times New Roman, 12 pt. or Calibri, 11 pt.

- **Use white, ivory, or light-colored paper.** Gray or tan paper is acceptable. Use standard-size paper (8.5" x 11") for a printed resume.

EMPLOYMENT APPLICATION (COVER) LETTER

A one-page application letter (cover letter) should accompany every resume. (See p. 45 for a model application letter.) This letter should include the following three topics in three to five paragraphs:

- **Specify position.** The first paragraph should include the position applied for and how you learned of the opening.

- **Include qualifications.** In one to three paragraphs, include evidence that you qualify for the position. Interpret information presented in the accompanying resume to show how your qualifications relate to the specified job.

- **Request an interview.** The last paragraph should request an interview and give precise information for contacting you to arrange it.

APPLICATION FORM

Many companies require an applicant to complete an employment application form even though a resume and application letter have been received. Provide information that is accurate, complete, legible, and neat. You should carry a copy of your resume when applying in person or going to an interview. Much of the information requested on the application form can be copied efficiently and accurately from the resume. See p. 46 for an illustration of an application form.

INTERVIEW FOLLOW-UP LETTER

Within 24 hours following a job interview, you should send a follow-up letter thanking the interviewer for the time and courtesies extended during the interview. This personal-business letter lets the interviewer know you are still interested in the job and reminds him/her of your qualifications. The interview follow-up also may be used to provide additional, relevant information about you. See p. 47 for a model follow-up letter.

Douglas H. Ruckert

8503 Kirby Drive
Houston TX 77054-8220
(713) 555-0121

dougr@suresend.com

OBJECTIVE: To use my computer, Internet, communication, and interpersonal skills in a challenging customer service position.

EDUCATION: Will graduate from Eisenhower Technical High School in June 2006, with a high school diploma and business technology emphasis. Grade point average is 3.75.

Relevant Skills and Courses:

- Proficient with most recent versions of Windows and Office, including Word, Excel, Access, PowerPoint, and FrontPage.

- Excelled in the following courses: Keyboarding, Computer Applications, Business Communications, and Office Technology.

Major Accomplishments:

- Future Business Leaders of America: Member for four years, vice president for one year. Won second place in Public Speaking at the District Competition; competed (same event) at state level.

- Varsity soccer: Lettered three years and served as captain during senior year.

- Recognition: Named one of Eisenhower's Top Ten Community Service Providers at end of junior year.

WORK EXPERIENCE: Hinton's Family Restaurant, Server (2005-present): Served customers in culturally diverse area, oriented new part-time employees, and resolved routine customer service issues.

Tuma's Landscape and Garden Center, Sales (2004-2005): Assisted customers with plant selection and responsible for stocking and arranging display areas.

REFERENCES: Will be furnished upon request.

Print Resume

Douglas H. Ruckert
8503 Kirby Drive
Houston TX 77054-8220
(713) 555-0121
dougr@suresend.com

SUMMARY

Strong communication and telephone skills; excellent keyboarding, computer, and Internet skills; and good organizational and interpersonal skills.

EDUCATION

Will graduate from Eisenhower Technical High School in June 2006, with a high school diploma and business technology emphasis. Grade point average is 3.75.

Relevant Skills and Courses:

Proficient with most recent versions of Windows and Office, including Word, Excel, Access, PowerPoint, and FrontPage.

Excelled in the following courses: Keyboarding, Computer Applications, Business Communications, and Office Technology.

Major Accomplishments:

Future Business Leaders of America: Member for four years, vice president for one year. Won second place in Public Speaking at District Competition; competed (same event) at state level.

Varsity soccer: Lettered three years and served as captain during senior year.

Recognition: Named one of Eisenhower's Top Ten Community Service Providers at end of junior year.

WORK EXPERIENCE

Hinton's Family Restaurant, Server (2005-present): Served customers in culturally diverse area, oriented new part-time employees, and resolved routine customer service issues.

Tuma's Landscape and Garden Center, Sales (2004-2005): Assisted customers with plant selection and responsible for stocking and arranging display areas.

REFERENCES

Will be furnished upon request.

Electronic Resume

8503 Kirby Drive
Houston, TX 77054-8220
May 10, 2006

Ms. Jenna St. John
Personnel Director
Regency Insurance Company
219 West Greene Road
Houston, TX 77067-4219

Dear Ms. St. John:

Ms. Anne D. Salgado, my business technology instructor, informed me of the customer service position with your company that will be available June 15. She speaks very highly of your organization. After learning more about the position, I am confident that I am qualified and would like to be considered for the position.

Currently I am completing my senior year at Eisenhower Technical High School. All of my elective courses have been computer and business-related courses. I have completed the advanced computer application class where we integrated word processing, spreadsheet, database, presentation, and Web page documents by using the latest suite software. I have also taken an office technology course that included practice in using the telephone and applying interpersonal skills.

My work experience and school activities have given me the opportunity to work with people to achieve group goals. Participating in FBLA has given me an appreciation of the business world.

The opportunity to interview with you for this position will be greatly appreciated. You can call me at (713) 555-0121 or e-mail me at <u>dougr@suresend.com</u> to arrange an interview.

Sincerely,

Douglas H. Ruckert

Enclosure

Application Letter

Application for Employment
Regency Insurance Company

An Equal Opportunity Employer

PERSONAL INFORMATION

NAME (LAST FIRST)	SOCIAL SECURITY NO.	CURRENT DATE	PHONE NUMBER
Ruckert, Douglas H.	368-56-2890	5/22/06	(713) 555-0121

ADDRESS (NUMBER, STREET, CITY, STATE, ZIP CODE)	U.S. CITIZEN	DATE YOU CAN START
8503 Kirby Dr., Houston, TX 77054-8220	☒ YES ☐ NO	6/10/06

ARE YOU EMPLOYED NOW?	IF YES, MAY WE INQUIRE OF YOUR PRESENT EMPLOYER?	IF YES, GIVE NAME AND NUMBER OF PERSON TO CALL
☒ YES ☐ NO	☒ YES ☐ NO	James Veloski, Manager (713) 555-0182

POSITION DESIRED	SALARY DESIRED	STATE HOW YOU LEARNED OF POSITION
Customer Service	Open	From Ms. Anne D. Salgado Eisenhower Business Technology Instructor

HAVE YOU EVER BEEN CONVICTED OF A FELONY?
☐ YES ☒ NO   IF YES, EXPLAIN.

EDUCATION

	NAME AND LOCATION OF SCHOOL	YEARS ATTENDED	DID YOU GRADUATE?	SUBJECTS STUDIED
COLLEGE				
HIGH SCHOOL	Eisenhower Technical High School Houston, TX	2002 to 2006	Will graduate 06/06	Business Technology
GRADE SCHOOL				
OTHER				

SUBJECTS OF SPECIAL STUDY/RESEARCH WORK OR SPECIAL TRAINING/SKILLS DIRECTLY RELATED TO POSITION DESIRED

Windows and Office Suite, including Word, Excel, Access, PowerPoint, and FrontPage

Office Procedures course with telephone training and interpersonal skills role playing

FORMER EMPLOYERS (LIST LAST POSITION FIRST)

FROM - TO (MTH & YEAR)	NAME AND ADDRESS	SALARY	POSITION	REASON FOR LEAVING
9/05 to present	Hinton's Family Restaurant, 2204 S. Wayside Avenue, Houston, TX 77023-8841	$6.85/hr.	Server	Want full-time position in my field
6/04 to 9/05	Tuma's Landscape and Garden Center 10155 East Freeway, Houston, TX 77029-4419	$5.75/hr.	Sales	Employed at Hinton's

REFERENCES (LIST THREE PERSONS NOT RELATED TO YOU, WHOM YOU HAVE KNOWN AT LEAST ONE YEAR)

NAME	BUSINESS ADDRESS	PHONE NUMBER	TITLE	YEARS KNOWN
Ms. Anne D. Salgado	Eisenhower Technical High School, 100 W. Cavalcade, Houston, TX 77009-2451	(713) 555-0134	Business Technology Instructor	Four
Mr. James R. Veloski	Hinton's Family Restaurant, 2204 S. Wayside Avenue, Houston, TX 77023-8841	(713) 555-0182	Manager	One
Mrs. Helen T. Landis	Tuma's Landscape and Garden Center, 10155 East Freeway, Houston, TX 77029-4419	(713) 555-0149	Owner	Three

I UNDERSTAND THAT I SHALL NOT BECOME AN EMPLOYEE UNTIL I HAVE SIGNED AN EMPLOYMENT AGREEMENT WITH THE FINAL APPROVAL OF THE EMPLOYER AND THAT SUCH EMPLOYMENT WILL BE SUBJECT TO VERIFICATION OF PREVIOUS EMPLOYMENT DATA PROVIDED IN THIS APPLICATION, ANY RELATED DOCUMENTS, OR DATA SHEET. I KNOW THAT A REPORT MAY BE MADE THAT WILL INCLUDE INFORMATION CONCERNING ANY FACTOR THE EMPLOYER MIGHT FIND RELEVANT TO THE POSITION FOR WHICH I AM APPLYING, AND THAT I CAN MAKE A WRITTEN REQUEST FOR ADDITIONAL INFORMATION AS TO THE NATURE AND SCOPE OF THE REPORT IF ONE IS MADE.

Douglas H. Ruckert
SIGNATURE OF APPLICANT

Employment Application Form

8503 Kirby Drive
Houston, TX 77054-8220
May 25, 2006

Ms. Jenna St. John
Personnel Director
Regency Insurance Company
219 West Greene Road
Houston, TX 77067-4219

Dear Ms. St. John:

Thank you for discussing the customer service opening at Regency Insurance Company. I have a much better understanding of the position after meeting with you and Mr. Meade.

Mr. Meade was extremely helpful in explaining the specific job responsibilities. My previous jobs and my business technology classes required me to complete many of the tasks that he mentioned. With minimal training, I believe I could be an asset to your company.

Even though I realize it will be a real challenge to replace a person like Mr. Meade, it is a challenge that I will welcome. If there is further information that would be helpful as you consider my application, please let me know.

Sincerely,

Douglas H. Ruckert

Follow-up Letter

Style Guide

CAPITALIZATION GUIDES

CAPITALIZE

1. The first word of every sentence and complete quotation. Do not capitalize (a) fragments of quotations or (b) a quotation resumed within a sentence.

   > Crazy Horse said, "I will return to you in stone."
   > Ghandi's teaching inspired "nonviolent revolutions."
   > "It is . . . fitting and proper," Lincoln said, "that we . . . do this."

2. The first word after a colon if that word begins a complete sentence.

   > Remember: Keep the action in your fingers.
   > These sizes were in stock: small, medium, and extra large.

3. First, last, and all other words in titles except articles, conjunctions, or prepositions of four or fewer letters.

   > *The Beak of the Finch*
   > *Raleigh News and Observer*
   > "The Phantom of the Opera"

4. An official title when it precedes a name or when used elsewhere if it is a title of distinction.

   > In what year did Juan Carlos become King of Spain?
   > Masami Chou, our class president, met Senator Thurmond.

5. Personal titles and names of people and places.

   > Did you see Mrs. Watts and Gloria while in Miami?

6. All proper nouns and their derivatives.

   > Mexico   Mexican border   Uganda   Ugandan economy

7. Days of the week, months of the year, holidays, periods of history, and historic events.

   > Friday   July   Labor Day
   > Middle Ages   Vietnam War   Woodstock

8. Geographic regions, localities, and names.

   > the East Coast   Upper Peninsula Michigan
   > Ohio River   the Deep South

9. Street, avenue, company, etc., when used with a proper noun.

   > Fifth Avenue   Wall Street   Monsanto Company

10. Names of organizations, clubs, and buildings.

    > National Hockey League   Four-H Club
    > Biltmore House   Omni Hotel

11. A noun preceding a figure except for common nouns, such as line, page, and sentence.

    Review Rules 1 to 18 in Chapter 5, page 149.

12. Seasons of the year only when they are personified.

    the soft kiss of Spring   the icy fingers of Winter

NUMBER EXPRESSION GUIDES

USE WORDS FOR

1. Numbers from one to ten except when used with numbers above ten, which are keyed as figures. Common business practice is to use figures for all numbers except those that begin a sentence.

    Did you visit all eight Web sites, or only four?
    Buy 15 textbooks and 8 workbooks.

2. A number beginning a sentence.

    Twelve of the new shrubs have died; 48 are doing well.

3. The shorter of two numbers used together.

    fifty 42-cent stamps   150 twenty-cent stamps

4. Isolated fractions or indefinite numbers in a sentence.

    Nearly seventy members voted, which is almost one-fourth.

5. Names of small-numbered streets and avenues (ten and under).

    The theater is at the corner of Third Avenue and 54th Street.

USE FIGURES FOR

1. Dates and times except in very formal writing.

    The flight will arrive at 9:48 a.m. on March 14.
    The ceremony took place the fifth of June at eleven o'clock.

2. A series of fractions and/or mixed numbers.

    Key 1/4, 1/2, 5/6, and 7 3/4.

3. Numbers following nouns.

    Case 1849 is reviewed in Volume 5, page 9.

4. Measures, weights, and dimensions.

    6 feet 9 inches   7 pounds 4 ounces
    8.5 inches by 11 inches

5. Definite numbers used with percent (%), but use words for indefinite percentages.

    The late fee is 15 percent of the overdue payment.
    The brothers put in nearly fifty percent of the start-up capital.

6. House numbers except house number *One*.

> My home is at 8 Weber Drive; my office is at One Weber Plaza.

7. Amounts of money except when spelled for emphasis (as in legal documents). Even amounts are keyed without the decimal. Large amounts (a million or more) are keyed as shown.

> $17.75 75 cents $775
> seven hundred dollars ($700)
> $7,500 $7 million $7.2 million $7 billion

PUNCTUATION GUIDES

USE AN APOSTROPHE

1. As a symbol for *feet* in charts, forms, and tables or as a symbol for *minutes*. (The quotation mark may be used as a symbol for *seconds* and *inches*.)

> 12' x 16' 3' 54" 8' 6" x 10' 8"

2. As a symbol to indicate the omission of letters or figures (as in contractions).

> can't do's and don'ts Class of '12

3. To form the plural of most figures, letters, and words used as words rather than for their meaning: Add the apostrophe and *s*. In market quotations and decades, form the plural of figures by the addition of *s* only.

> 7's ten's ABC's Century 4s 1960s

4. To show possession: Add the apostrophe and *s* to (a) a singular noun and (b) a plural noun that does not end in *s*.

> a woman's watch men's shoes girl's bicycle

Add the apostrophe and *s* to a proper name of one syllable that ends in *s*.

> Bess's Cafeteria James's hat Jones's bill

Add the apostrophe only after (a) plural nouns ending in *s* and (b) a proper name of more than one syllable that ends in *s* or *z*.

> girls' camp Adams' home Martinez' report

Add the apostrophe (and *s*) after the last noun in a series to indicate joint or common possession by two or more persons; however, add the possessive to each of the nouns to show separate possession by two or more persons.

> Lewis and Clark's expedition
> the secretary's and the treasurer's reports

USE A COLON

1. To introduce a listing.

> These poets are my favorites: Shelley, Keats, and Frost.

2. To introduce a question or a long direct quotation.

> The question is this: Did you study for the test?

3. Between hours and minutes expressed in figures.

> 10:15 a.m.   4:30 p.m.   12:00 midnight

Use a comma (or commas)

1. After (a) introductory phrases or clauses and (b) words in a series.

> When you finish keying the report, please give it to Mr. Kent.
> We will play the Mets, Expos, and Cubs in our next home stand.

2. To set off short direct quotations.

> Mrs. Ramirez replied, "No, the report is not finished."

3. Before and after (a) appositives—words that come together and refer to the same person, thing, or idea—and (b) words of direct address.

> Colette, the assistant manager, will chair the next meeting.
> Please call me, Erika, if I can be of further assistance.

4. To set off nonrestrictive clauses (not necessary to meaning of sentence), but not restrictive clauses (necessary to meaning).

> Your report, which deals with that issue, raised many questions.
> The man who organized the conference is my teacher.

5. To separate the day from the year in dates and the city from the state in addresses.

> July 4, 2012   St. Joseph, Missouri   Moose Point, AK

6. To separate two or more parallel adjectives (adjectives that modify the noun separately and that could be separated by the word *and* instead of the comma).

> The big, loud bully was ejected after he pushed the coach.
> The big, powerful car zoomed past the cheering crowd.
> Cynthia played a black lacquered grand piano at her concert.
> A small red fox squeezed through the fence to avoid the hounds.

7. To separate (a) unrelated groups of figures that occur together and (b) whole numbers into groups of three digits each. (Omit commas from years and page, policy, room, serial, and telephone numbers.)

> By the year 2010, 1,200 more local students will be enrolled.
> The supplies listed on Invoice #274068 are for Room 1953.

Use a dash

Create a dash by keying two hyphens or one em-dash.

1. For emphasis.

> The skater—in a clown costume—dazzled with fancy footwork.

2. To indicate a change of thought.

> We may tour the Orient—but I'm getting ahead of my story.

3. To emphasize the name of an author when it follows a direct quotation.

> "All the world's a stage . . . ."—Shakespeare

4. To set off expressions that break off or interrupt speech.

> "Jay, don't get too close to the—." I spoke too late.
> "Today—er—uh," the anxious presenter began.

USE AN EXCLAMATION POINT

1. After emphatic interjections.

> Wow!   Hey there!   What a day!

2. After sentences that are clearly exclamatory.

> "I won't go!" she said with determination.
> How good it was to see you in New Orleans last week!

USE A HYPHEN

1. To join parts of compound words expressing the numbers twenty-one through ninety-nine.

> Thirty-five delegates attended the national convention.

2. To join compound adjectives preceding a noun they modify as a unit.

> End-of-term grades will be posted on the classroom door.

3. After each word or figure in a series of words or figures that modify the same noun (suspended hyphenation).

> Meeting planners made first-, second-, and third-class reservations.

4. To spell out a word.

> The sign read, "For your c-o-n-v-i-e-n-c-e." Of course, the correct word is c-o-n-v-e-n-i-e-n-c-e.

5. To form certain compound nouns.

> WGAL-TV   spin-off   teacher-counselor   AFL-CIO

USE ITALIC

To indicate titles of books, magazines, and newspapers. (Titles may be keyed in ALL CAPS or underlined without the italic.)

> A review of *Runaway Jury* appeared in *The New York Times*.

USE PARENTHESES

1. To enclose parenthetical or explanatory matter and added information.

> Amendments to the bylaws (Exhibit A) are enclosed.

2. To enclose identifying letters or figures in a series.

   Check these factors: (1) period of time, (2) rate of pay, and (3) nature of duties.

3. To enclose figures that follow spelled-out amounts to give added clarity or emphasis.

   The total award is fifteen hundred dollars ($1,500).

USE A QUESTION MARK

1. At the end of a sentence that is a direct question. But use a period after requests in the form of a question (whenever the expected answer is action, not words).

   What has been the impact of the Information Superhighway?
   Will you complete the enclosed form and return it to me.

USE QUOTATION MARKS

1. To enclose direct quotations.

   Professor Dye asked, "Are you spending the summer in Europe?"
   Was it Emerson who said, "To have a friend is to be one"?

2. To enclose titles of articles, films/movies, plays, poems, songs, television programs, and unpublished works, such as theses and dissertations.

   "Matrix" with Keanu Reeves   "Fog" by Sandburg
   "Survivor" in prime time   "Memory" from "Cats"

3. To enclose special words or phrases or coined words (words not in dictionary usage).

   The words "phony" and "braggart" describe him, according to coworkers.
   The presenter annoyed the audience with phrases like "uh" and "you know."

USE A SEMICOLON

1. To separate two or more independent clauses in a compound sentence when the conjunction is omitted.

   Being critical is easy; being constructive is not so easy.

2. To separate independent clauses when they are joined by a conjunctive adverb, such as *consequently* or *therefore*.

   I work mornings; therefore, I prefer an afternoon interview.

3. To separate a series of phrases or clauses (especially if they contain commas) that are introduced by a colon.

   Al spoke in these cities: Denver, CO; Erie, PA; and Troy, NY.

4. To precede an abbreviation or word that introduces an explanatory statement.

   She organized her work; for example, naming folders and files to indicate degrees or urgency.

USE AN UNDERLINE

To call attention to words or phrases (or use quotation marks or italic).

   Take the presenter's advice: <u>Stand</u> up, <u>speak</u> up, and then <u>sit</u> down.
   Students often confuse <u>its</u> and <u>it's</u>.

BASIC GRAMMAR GUIDES

USE A SINGULAR VERB

1. With a singular subject.

   Dr. Cho was to give the lecture, but he is ill.

2. With indefinite pronouns (*each, every, any, either, neither, one,* etc.)

   Each of these girls has an important role in the class play.
   Neither of them is well enough to start the game.

3. With singular subjects linked by *or* or *nor*; but if one subject is singular and the other is plural, the verb agrees with the nearer subject.

   Neither Ms. Moss nor Mr. Katz was invited to speak.
   Either the manager or his assistants are to participate.

4. With a collective noun (*class, committee, family, team,* etc.) if the collective noun acts as a unit.

   The committee has completed its study and filed a report.
   The jury has returned to the courtroom to give its verdict.

5. With the pronouns *all* and *some* (as well as fractions and percentages) when used as subjects if their modifiers are singular. Use a plural verb if their modifiers are plural.

   Some of the new paint is already cracking and peeling.
   All of the workers are to be paid for the special holiday.
   Historically, about forty percent has voted.

6. When *number* is used as the subject and is preceded by *the*; use a plural verb if *number* is the subject and is preceded by *a*.

   The number of voters has increased again this year.
   A number of workers are on vacation this week.

USE A PLURAL VERB

1. With a plural subject.

   The players were all here, and they were getting restless.

2. With a compound subject joined by *and*.

   Mrs. Samoa and her son are to be on a local talk show.

NEGATIVE FORMS OF VERBS

1. Use the plural verb *do not* or *don't* with pronoun subjects *I, we, you,* and *they* as well as with plural nouns.

   I do not find this report believable; you don't either.

2. Use the singular verb *does not* or *doesn't* with pronouns *he, she,* and *it* as well as with singular nouns.

   Though she doesn't accept the board's offer, the board doesn't have to offer more.

PRONOUN AGREEMENT WITH ANTECEDENTS

1. A personal pronoun (*I, we, you, he, she, it, their*, etc.) agrees in person (first, second, or third) with the noun or other pronoun it represents.

   > We can win the game if we all give each play our best effort.
   > You may play softball after you finish your homework.
   > Andrea said that she will drive her car to the shopping mall.

2. A personal pronoun agrees in gender (feminine, masculine, or neuter) with the noun or other pronoun it represents.

   > Each winner will get a corsage as she receives her award.
   > Mr. Kimoto will give his talk after the announcements.
   > The small boat lost its way in the dense fog.

3. A personal pronoun agrees in number (singular or plural) with the noun or other pronoun it represents.

   > Celine drove her new car to Del Rio, Texas, last week.
   > The club officers made careful plans for their next meeting.

4. A personal pronoun that represents a collective noun (*team, committee, family*, etc.) may be singular or plural, depending on the meaning of the collective noun.

   > Our women's soccer team played its fifth game today.
   > The vice squad took their positions in the square.

COMMONLY CONFUSED PRONOUNS

it's (contraction): it is; it has
its (pronoun): possessive form of *it*

> It's good to get your e-mail; it's been a long time.
> The puppy wagged its tail in welcome.

their (pronoun): possessive form of *they*
there (adverb/pronoun): at or in that place; sometimes-used to introduce a sentence
they're (contraction): they are

> The hikers all wore their parkas.
> Will they be there during our presentation?
> They're likely to be late because of rush-hour traffic.

who's (contraction): who is; who has
whose (pronoun): possessive form of *who*

> Who's seen the movie? Who's going now?
> I chose the one whose skills are best.

CONFUSING WORDS

accept (vb) to receive; to approve; to take
except (prep/vb) with the exclusion of; leave out

affect (vb) to produce a change in or have an effect on
effect (n) result; something produced by an agent or a cause

buy (n/vb) to purchase; to acquire; a bargain
by (prep/adv) close to; via; according to; close at hand

choose (vb) to select; to decide
chose (vb) past tense of "choose"

cite (vb) use as support; commend; summon
sight (n/vb) ability to see; something seen; a device to improve aim
site (n) location

complement (n) something that fills, completes, or makes perfect
compliment (n/vb) a formal expression of respect or admiration; to pay respect or admiration

do (vb) to bring about; to carry out
due (adj) owed or owing as a debt; having reached the date for payment

farther (adv) greater distance
further (adv) additional; in greater depth; to greater extent

for (prep/conj) indicates purpose on behalf of; because of
four (n) two plus two in number

hear (vb) to gain knowledge of by the ear
here (adv) in or at this place; at or on this point; in this case

hole (n) opening in or through something
whole (adj/n) having all its proper parts; a complete amount

hour (n) the 24th part of a day; a particular time
our (adj) possessive form of "we"; of or relating to us

knew (vb) past tense of "know"; understood; recognized truth or nature of
new (adj) novel; fresh; existing for a short time

know (vb) to be aware of the truth or nature of; to have an understanding of
no (adv/adj/n) not in any respect or degree; not so; indicates denial or refusal

lessen (vb) to cause to decrease; to make less
lesson (n) something to be learned; period of instruction; a class period

lie (n/vb) an untrue or inaccurate statement; to tell an untrue story; to rest or recline
lye (n) a strong alkaline substance or solution

one (adj/pron) a single unit or thing
won (vb) past tense of win; gained a victory as in a game or contest; got by effort or work

passed (vb) past tense of "pass"; already occurred; moved by; gave an item to someone
past (adv/adj/prep/n) gone or elapsed; time gone by

personal (adj) of, relating to, or affecting a person; done in person
personnel (n) a staff or persons making up a workforce in an organization

plain (adj/n) with little decoration; a large flat area of land
plane (n) an airplane or hydroplane

pole (n) a long, slender, rounded piece of wood or other material
poll (n) a survey of people to analyze public opinion

principal (n/adj) a chief or leader; capital (money) amount placed at interest; of or relating to the most important thing or matter or persons
principle (n) a central rule, law, or doctrine

right (adj) factual; true; correct
rite (n) customary form of ceremony; ritual
write (v) to form letters or symbols; to compose and set down in words, numbers, or symbols

some (n/adv) unknown or unspecified unit or thing; to a degree or extent
sum (n/vb) total; to find a total; to summarize

stationary (adj) fixed in a position, course, or mode; unchanging in condition
stationery (n) paper and envelopes used for processing personal and business documents

than (conj/prep) used in comparisons to show differences between items
then (n/adv) that time; at that time; next

to (prep/adj) indicates action, relation, distance, direction
too (adv) besides; also; to excessive degree
two (n/adj) one plus one

vary (vb) change; make different; diverge
very (adv/adj) real; mere; truly; to high degree

waist (n) narrowed part of the body between chest and hips; middle of something
waste (n/vb/adj) useless things; rubbish; spend or use carelessly; nonproductive

weak (adj) lacking strength, skill, or proficiency
week (n) a series of seven days; Monday through Sunday

wear (vb/n) to bear or have on the person; diminish by use; clothing
where (adv/conj/n) at, in, or to what degree; what place, source, or cause

your (adj) of or relating to you as possessor
you're (contraction) you are

PROOFREADERS' MARKS

Proofreaders' marks are used to mark corrections in keyed or printed text that contains problems and/or errors. As a keyboard user, you should be able to read these marks accurately when revising or editing a rough draft. You also should be able to write these symbols to correct the rough drafts that you and others key. The most-used proofreaders' marks are shown below.

‖	Align copy; also, make these items parallel	#>	Insert space
¶	Begin a new paragraph	∨	Insert apostrophe
Cap ≡	Capitalize	stet	Let it stand; ignore correction
◡	Close up	lc	Lowercase
ℓ	Delete	⎵	Move down; lower
⊂#	Delete space	⊏	Move left
No ¶	Do not begin a new paragraph	⊐	Move right
∧	Insert	⌐⌐	Move up; raise
⌄	Insert comma	sp	Spell out
⊙	Insert period	tr	Transpose
∨∨	Insert quotation marks	———	Underline or italic

Index

Note: **Boldface** numbers indicate illustrations.